# Unnerved

# Unnerved

## The Performer's Guide to Managing Anxiety

Melissa Plamann

BLOOMSBURY ACADEMIC
NEW YORK • LONDON • OXFORD • NEW DELHI • SYDNEY

BLOOMSBURY ACADEMIC

Bloomsbury Publishing Inc, 1359 Broadway, New York, NY 10018, USA
Bloomsbury Publishing Plc, 50 Bedford Square, London, WC1B 3DP, UK
Bloomsbury Publishing Ireland, 29 Earlsfort Terrace, Dublin 2, D02 AY28, Ireland

BLOOMSBURY, BLOOMSBURY ACADEMIC and the Diana logo are trademarks of
Bloomsbury Publishing Plc

First published in the United States of America 2025

Copyright © Melissa Plamann, 2025

For legal purposes the Acknowledgments on p. 151 constitute an extension of
this copyright page.

Cover design: Sally Rinehart
Cover image © Stefan Prodanovic

All rights reserved. No part of this publication may be: i) reproduced or transmitted in any form, electronic or mechanical, including photocopying, recording or by means of any information storage or retrieval system without prior permission in writing from the publishers; or ii) used or reproduced in any way for the training, development or operation of artificial intelligence (AI) technologies, including generative AI technologies. The rights holders expressly reserve this publication from the text and data mining exception as per Article 4(3) of the Digital Single Market Directive (EU) 2019/790.

Bloomsbury Publishing Inc does not have any control over, or responsibility for, any third-party websites referred to or in this book. All internet addresses given in this book were correct at the time of going to press. The author and publisher regret any inconvenience caused if addresses have changed or sites have ceased to exist, but can accept no responsibility for any such changes.

Library of Congress Cataloging-in-Publication Data Available

ISBN: HB: 979-8-2163-6633-1
PB: 979-8-2163-6634-8
ePub: 979-8-2163-5234-1
ePDF: 979-8-2163-5235-8

Typeset by Deanta Global Publishing Services, Chennai, India
Printed and bound in the United States of America

For product safety related questions contact productsafety@bloomsbury.com.

To find out more about our authors and books visit www.bloomsbury.com and
sign up for our newsletters.

# Contents

Prologue: It's Complicated  vii

1  The Problem: Anatomy of Performance Anxiety  1

2  Help: Medication, Therapy, and Other Options  17

3  Solid Ground: The Enneagram  39

4  Shame: The Feeling Triad (Helpers, Achievers, and Individualists)  49

5  Fear: The Thinking Triad (Investigators, Loyalists, and Enthusiasts)  63

6  Anger: The Doing Triad (Reformers, Challengers, and Peacemakers)  79

7  Nine Lives: Performance Anxiety and the Enneagram  95

8  Letting Go: The Mind-Body Connection  107

9  Why Me?: Cultural Baggage Impacting Anxiety  119

10  Assembling the Toolkit: Preparation and Performance  133

Epilogue: It's Still Complicated  145
Acknowledgments  151
References  153
Index  159

# Prologue
## It's Complicated

I don't love performing. Many people might concur, but I am a performer by training and trade. So, when I dare utter those words aloud, I'm met with surprise, or dismay, or disbelief, or even abject disappointment from colleagues and friends. But I believe if many performers are truly honest with themselves, they'll find a complicated relationship with this thing we call "performance." It may be our calling, our passion, or simply our chosen career, but our feelings about performing are often complex, forged over a lifetime of individual moments onstage and off. Very often, the unwelcome elephant in the performance hall is anxiety, and we assign to it the power to impact our beliefs about our talent, our worth, and our ability to perform. For many years, it terrified me and caused me to hate performing altogether.

Like many performers, I spent the bulk of my musical training tiptoeing around performance anxiety. I tried to rationalize my way out of actually feeling the percolating in my stomach, the tightening of my jaw, the heat in my ears, the pounding in my chest. After all, I was *ready*. I had over-rehearsed. I had bargained with the Universe (*Just let me play well this ONE time, and I will x, y, z for eternity.*) I read all the books and took the quizzes. I highlighted passages and reread *The Inner Game of Music* ad nauseam. I prayed and meditated and read calming poetry. I pretended to *embrace* the performance anxiety (*Hello, Old Friend! I see we meet again!*). But in the end, I would stand just offstage, with a beta-blocker dissolving under my tongue, hoping against hope that things would go well, but feeling utterly, wildly, out of control.

My breaking point came after I had been awarded a doctorate in performance from a highly regarded music school and had several years of collegiate teaching under my belt. Not only was I a performer myself, but I was teaching performers! I had calligraphed diplomas declaring me a *professional* at this performing thing. With these credentials and some friends in the right places, I was invited to my undergraduate alma mater to perform a Distinguished Alumni solo recital. All of my mentors and past professors were there; current and former students came in droves (or, at least small handfuls). Family flew in to attend. I was petrified.

I progressed through the first few pieces in a terrified blur; they went well enough, but I was barely present. I looked out into the sea of revered faces, and while I bowed with a forced smile, I thought, "Ohmygod, Ohmygod, Ohmygod." Then came the most technically demanding piece, thoughtfully positioned about a third of the way through: far enough in to have gotten out the initial nerves, but not so late in the program for stamina to have waned. What happened next had not ever happened before, nor has it happened since: I lost my place. For one terrifying, this-is-the-end-of-my-career moment, time stood still and the air hung with complete, deafening silence. My mind was blank, and my body responded with an immediate rush of adrenaline; I heard my pulse whooshing in my ears, and I tasted iron. It felt like an entire lifetime condensed into what must have been only a few seconds before I could find the musical line and get back into the piece. My body felt like rubber, as though I had run a marathon in that time gap. Somehow, I completed the rest of the program with nearly flawless performances of the remaining pieces. But, I was gone. I had lost myself completely.

Afterward, I could not comprehend the gross disconnect between my experience and the audience's. People applauded uproariously. *Did they feel sorry for me?* I was enveloped in hugs and received accolades. *Did they experience the same concert I experienced? The one where my career exploded before my eyes? The one where I unraveled and never recovered?* Finally, my undergraduate professor, who is now a close friend, came to congratulate me and I begged of her, "What about the Bach? When I got lost?" She seemed to suddenly remember and said, "Oh yeah. I wondered what happened. It didn't ruin anything—you handled it like a pro!" I was astounded. I wanted to run to the nearest bridge and jump right off. I wanted to become an accountant and never step foot under the bright lights again (no offense to accountants). I simply didn't understand.

To make matters worse, the next day I was to speak in a masterclass to the performance majors. The topic, you ask? *Performance Anxiety*. On the heels of what felt like an inward struggle-to-the-death with this personal demon (I lost, if it wasn't already painfully clear), I now found myself armed with ridiculous handouts touting fluffy mental exercises and affirming self-talk. I gave an hour-long class on how to deal with anxiety while feeling like the biggest fraud alive—Imposter Syndrome at its finest. If I had been further away from this life-altering event, I like to think I would have given a different, more honest masterclass. But the truth is, I shoved this experience deep down and tried to forget it ever happened. I dealt with it like I dealt with every other negative experience and emotion—through denial, manic work, a rededication to perfectionism, and lots of other destructive habits, like a worsening of a decades-long danse macabre with an eating disorder.

Many performers have publicly admitted to struggling with performance anxiety. For some, like Barbara Streisand, it has been crippling at certain stages. Others, like pop icons Adele and Taylor Swift, have spoken about stage fright popping up even after staggering professional triumphs. Studies suggest that anywhere from 60 percent to 95 percent of professional musicians suffer from performance anxiety severe enough to adversely impact their performances.[1, 2] It seems that this proverbial elephant simply will not take leave of our performing spaces; so, what are we to do?

Perhaps it is my misinterpretation, but the message I internalized during my musical upbringing was that my teachers were to teach technique, musicality, technical issues, repertoire... but it was *my* job to deal with my internal demons. The advice I read and received was simple: *welcome* performance anxiety and be *grateful* for its presence. It means you *care* about your art, and it gives you that intangible *edge* while performing. I even passed on this advice to students for a long time, even though it always felt like a load of bullshit to me. Frankly, this advice—and a lot of the practical tricks (some of which are incredibly useful!) found in existing books on performance anxiety—seem to treat the symptoms, rather than the underlying causes, of this chronic condition.

If you are a magical unicorn performer who can truly look performance anxiety in the eye and welcome it on the performing journey, opening the door for it to take a backseat during the ride and thanking it for its presence, this book is not for you. But if you have already read the books, taken the quizzes, surrendered to the Universe, and breathed in so many box counts that you have nearly hyperventilated, and you *still* see the damn elephant in every performance hall (or sports arena, or boardroom, or . . .), then I invite you to continue this journey of exploring your personal relationship with performing and commence some challenging work that will help you manage your anxiety, given your unique personality and situation.

Over the last several years, I undertook a lot of intentional work to better understand and manage my own anxiety. I did not realize I was actually researching to write this book. I tried different types of meditation, medication, exercise, and therapy. I researched hormonal imbalances, mindfulness, and exactly how adrenaline works in the body. I explored the world of personality typing and delved into the wisdom of the enneagram. I listened to endless podcasts and read piles of books on topics ranging from psychosomatic pain to sobriety, menopause to diet culture. Over the course of this journey, I arrived at answers—and lots more questions—that have helped me in my chronic struggle with performance anxiety. While every performer is unique, I believe these discoveries can also help you.

Many studies confirm that performance anxiety begins in adolescence and persists for most musicians throughout their lives. It is markedly worse among student groups, and it most affects professional musicians under the age of forty-five. This book is designed particularly for those groups—students and young(ish) professional musicians. However, anxiety persists for most musicians even into later years, and certain life events like menopause can amplify anxiety. So, this book is for anyone who experiences performance anxiety of any kind, at any age. Because I am a musician, I primarily refer to music performance anxiety; that is my lived experience. However, all of the information in this book can easily be applied to performers more widely, as performances take place everywhere, every day—sports arenas, conference rooms, TV studios, dance halls, church pulpits, and so on.

I finally decided to write this book when, in a single week, all of the following happened:

- A former student called in tears, asking for help with performance anxiety as they prepared a graduate recital.
- A seventy-two-year-old student (she'd studied music in college but then pursued a career in communications and returned to music in retirement) said to me before a studio class, "I'm shaking like a leaf. I assumed at seventy-two I wouldn't be so nervous anymore!"

- My own former professor, now retired, had been featured in a recital honoring *her* professor at the end of his life. She told me about the performance, which went well, but said, "It never goes away. The nerves just never go away."
- A current student underperformed in a casual lunchtime recital. Afterward, as we discussed it, he said, "I was just scared. My nerves got the best of me."

In all of these scenarios, I wanted to offer more than empathy and an understanding pat on the back. I wished I knew more about performance anxiety and could give them a resource outlining why and how anxiety attacks, what the root causes are, and how we could better manage the nerves in ways that would work for each of our unique personalities.

This book is designed to help you uncover what makes *you* tick as a performer. You will discover that not all chapters are equally helpful for you—feel free to skip the ones that are not. After taking an objective look at what we mean by "performance anxiety," we will look at treatment options, including medication and therapy. Then, we will delve into our own personal responses to anxiety as they are governed by the ancient enneagram system. Even if you do not embrace the enneagram model entirely (I get it—I rolled my eyes *hard* the first time I heard of it), I find it helpful to examine the broad characteristics of our personalities, which can inform what compels our feelings and behaviors. We will find that the driver for performance anxiety is one of three major emotions particular to our enneagram type: fear, shame, or anger. Once we determine our root emotional drivers, we can address our unique brands of performance anxiety and dig into the rewarding work of managing it.

In later chapters, we will examine the role of the Covid-19 pandemic on anxiety and performance, especially with the rise of live streams and recording technology that freeze a performance in online perpetuity. We will also address the cultural baggage many of us carry, making our performing burden even heavier—things like hierarchical relationships, educational settings, hormone shifts, and even gender. Finally, we will look at what successful performance preparation and execution might look like through the lens of this new information.

Each chapter ends with some questions and activities for self-reflection. If these seem frivolous or unhelpful to you, don't do them. But, if you can set aside mental energy and time for this sort of reflection, I would urge you to begin a new journal dedicated to this journey of understanding yourself as a performer. Choose one or more questions that spark curiosity (or any emotion) and write on those. By the end of this book, you'll be equipped with a comprehensive narrative about your own performing journey and work to do that will help you face your personal performing demons. Elephants. Whatever—I can't decide on the better metaphor.

## *Questions for Reflection:*

- What has your experience with performance anxiety been throughout your life? Create a narrative detailing your relationship with performance up to this point.
- Make a timeline of your performance journey, and include the highs and lows of your performance anxiety. (Note that this may differ from others' perceptions of the performances themselves.)
- What has been the lowest point for you in terms of performance anxiety?
- What are the rituals, activities, or practices that have effectively tempered your performance anxiety?
- What techniques have been unhelpful for you in dealing with performance anxiety?
- How much time and/or resources have you devoted to managing your performance anxiety?
- What has been your most satisfying performance? What level of anxiety accompanied this event?

## Notes

**1** Jacy A. Cina, "Music Performance Anxiety and Cognitive-Behavioral Therapy: Some Pedagogical Insights," *College Music Symposium* 61, no. 2 (Fall 2021): 53.

**2** Belén Gómez-López and Roberto Sánchez-Cabrero, "Current Trends in Music Performance Anxiety Intervention," *Behavioral Science* 13 (2023): 720.

# 1 The Problem
## *Anatomy of Performance Anxiety*

If you picked up this book, you probably don't need an entire chapter dedicated to defining performance anxiety. You know it intimately; your body feels it in a primal way. It may present as trembling hands or hot ears, sweaty palms or an adrenaline rush right to the heart. However it finds purchase in your particular body and mind, you most certainly have a checklist by which you can identify performance anxiety. But for the sake of establishing some common ground, let's look first at the prevalence of performance anxiety; then, we will delve into the physiology of anxiety. If we want to understand our anxiety and find ways to alter or influence it, we need to learn where and how it manifests, and why it is called to action. Perhaps more interestingly, we also need to learn *whom* performance anxiety affects (spoiler alert: the number is likely higher than you think.)

## The Data

In 2021, I read an article in the *College Music Symposium* that blew my mind. While I anecdotally understand that "most" musicians suffer from some degree of performance anxiety, I had never encountered such compelling statistics regarding its prevalence and damage. In "Music Performance Anxiety and Cognitive-Behavioral Therapy," Jacy Cina begins by addressing the elephant in the room, stating that while performance anxiety recently occupies more space within the academic sphere, "most musicians prefer to avoid [admitting it] due to fear of judgment."[1] Hear, hear! Cina utilizes multiple studies, ranging from the 1980s through early 2000s, which all suggest that performance anxiety tends to manifest in adolescence and continues for many musicians throughout their performing careers.

Performance anxiety is a documented mental health issue with which most musicians struggle. While we may feel embarrassed or sense that our peers or colleagues do not feel the same level of anxiety, the data suggest otherwise. We do not do ourselves (or others) justice when we ignore it or downplay its severity. Performance anxiety can lead to depression, addiction, or other harmful coping mechanisms, and it can lead musicians to quit music altogether. I would encourage everyone to read the full article by Jacy Cina, which cites multiple noteworthy studies; the data below comes from several of them.[2] Here are some of the statistics that really stand out:

- In one major study, the top three symptoms of performance anxiety were:
  - rapid heartbeat (67 percent)
  - sweating hands (56 percent)
  - muscle tension (56 percent)
- Other symptoms included:
  - shortness of breath
  - nausea
  - dizziness
  - trembling hands
- Behavioral disturbances included:
  - avoiding performances
  - backing out of performance commitments

This is serious stuff. I would challenge anyone to find a physician who would brush off these symptoms. If a patient presents with increased heart rate and perspiration, tense muscles, nausea, and dizziness, any medical practitioner would be concerned and suggest treatment. Likewise, if something causes behavioral changes, it must be addressed. One of the questions on any intake form about pain or injury asks whether said malady interrupts normal daily life. In the case of performance anxiety, it is clear that the condition causes significant disruption and sometimes results in behavioral shifts. Performance anxiety is so serious that the American Psychological Association classifies it as "a subset of, and even precursor to, social anxiety disorder."[3] I daresay that if a friend were suffering from another ailment defined by the American Psychological Association, we would not simply urge them to breathe more intentionally and visualize their way out of the disorder. We would demand that they seek professional help, and possibly medication.

Dr. Dianna T. Kenny, former professor of psychology and music at the University of Sydney in Australia, has conducted extensive research on music performance anxiety. She proposed a new, comprehensive definition in 2009:

> Music performance anxiety is the experience of marked and persistent anxious apprehension related to musical performance that has arisen through specific anxiety conditioning experiences and which is manifested through combinations of affective, cognitive, somatic and behavioural symptoms. It may occur in a range of performance settings, but is usually more severe in settings involving high ego investment and evaluative threat. It may be focal (i.e. focused only on music performance), or occur comorbidly with other anxiety disorders, in particular social phobia. It affects musicians across the lifespan and is at least partially independent of years of training, practice and level of musical accomplishment. It may or may not impair the quality of the musical performance.[4]

This definition synthesizes findings from many studies, all proving that performance anxiety is nearly universal and often is a lifelong ailment.

Most performers can relate to this definition. When we perceive high levels of "evaluative threat," such as a jury or audition, anxiety increases. While we might hope performance anxiety will abate simply with age or experience, it likely will not. Importantly, Kenny concludes that anxiety may not actually impact the perceived quality of a performance. In the Prologue, I related my own performance anxiety attack in the middle of a recital; afterward, I could not comprehend the disconnect between my experience and the audience's. My internal struggle had not been obvious to them and had not impacted their perception of the performance's quality, even though I felt overwhelmed onstage. This definition explains the disparate elements of performance anxiety and its impact on performers' physical, emotional, and mental states.

In 2023, Belén Gómez-López and Roberto Sánchez-Cabrero published an eye-opening review compiling new music performance anxiety research from 2018 to 2023. Here are some staggering statistics from this review:[5]

- One study indicated that *60 percent to 80 percent* of professional musicians suffer from "debilitating" performance anxiety.[6]
- Another found that *95 percent* of participants experienced stage anxiety during live performances.[7]
- A study of over 560 musicians and 60 teachers showed that *one in three* musicians suffer from performance anxiety.[8]
- *Twenty percent* of students who choose to leave music do so because of performance anxiety.[9]

*Anywhere from 60 percent to 95 percent of musicians experience performance anxiety.* While I had always suspected that "most" performers are impacted by anxiety, these numbers prove that an incredibly high majority suffer from it.

A 1997 study by the Fédération Internationale des Musiciens remains one of the largest on music performance anxiety. Professional orchestral musicians from fifty-six orchestras throughout the world were surveyed, and they reported the symptoms of performance anxiety listed earlier. This study found that 70 percent of professional musicians suffered from performance anxiety severe enough to impact their performances. The finding that seven out of ten professional musicians experience performance anxiety severe enough to negatively affect their performances should raise some serious red flags. For any teachers or conductors out there: this means that (at least) 70 percent of your musicians are (by their perception) not performing to their peak ability. For performers: this means that you are in VERY good company. This is not a deep, dark personal flaw only afflicting you. It's the norm even among professionals.

While 70 percent is a high majority, I am inclined to believe the actual number is closer to the 95 percent suggested by the more recent 2022 study. In over fifteen years of collegiate teaching, I have spoken freely with my students about performance anxiety. I ask them to take the temperature of their anxiety frequently, and I inquire about the tools and tricks they intend to utilize during performance. I check in with them before performances and offer advice I suspect will work for their particular personalities. In my tenure, I have only encountered one student who claimed not to suffer from performance anxiety—he is an anomaly. Likewise, the more I admit my own struggles with performance anxiety, the more I learn from colleagues and peers that they too suffer from it, to varying degrees.

Cina cites another study from 1987, which reveals the following:

> [Steptoe and Fidler's] findings indicated higher levels of performance anxiety among students compared with professional musicians, and within the group of professionals, MPA [music performance anxiety] was negatively correlated with age and amount of performance experience. Initially, these results appear to demonstrate that repeated exposure to performance settings leads to a reduction in MPA levels. However, Steptoe and Fidler suggest that these results could also reflect that high-MPA musicians may become so overwhelmed by the pressures of a competitive orchestra job that they give up early in their career.[10]

These findings should give us all pause. Other studies suggest the onset of performance anxiety is likely during adolescence, when adolescents are particularly susceptible to self-critique.[11] This means that teachers—particularly those of young students—should explicitly address performance anxiety and suggest professional assistance for this mental health issue affecting the majority of musicians.

Recent studies[12] report that 20 percent of students who leave music do so because of performance anxiety. The music profession has undoubtedly lost valuable members to this mental health issue; I have watched some of my own promising students take positions requiring less performing in order to alleviate the "overwhelming pressures" of this field. Even during my own doctoral studies, I contemplated quitting music several times, and once actually did (more on that later).

## The Brain

Now that we've established that performance anxiety affects most musicians, let's look at exactly *how* this anxiety manifests and results in the symptoms described by so many performers. As you may have guessed, our entire experience of performance anxiety is controlled by the brain. The human brain is a complex mechanism that remains mysterious even to top neuroscientists

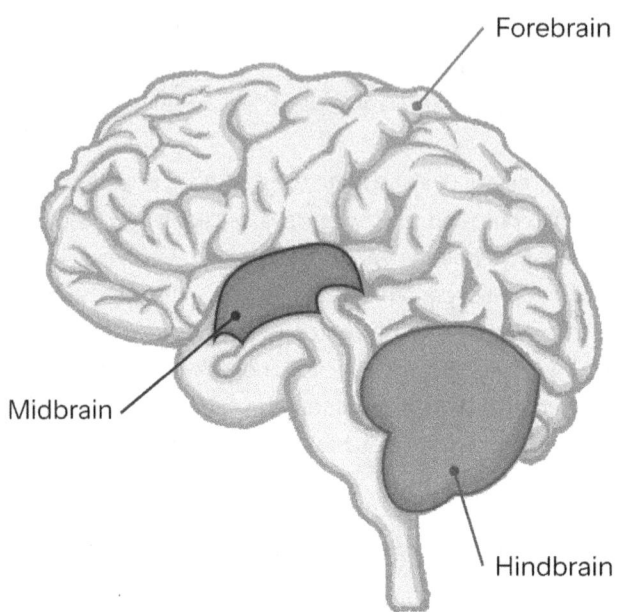

**Figure 1.1 The three large divisions of the brain.**

who dedicate their careers to its study. The simplest way we can discuss the brain is by dissecting it into three major regions (See Figure 1.1):

1. The forebrain
2. The midbrain
3. The hindbrain[13]

These three regions contain many different parts, which control different areas and store different information. A performance—whether on a stage, at a sports arena, or in a conference room—requires many separate parts of the brain working together. In the most general terms, the forebrain is responsible for sensory processing, reasoning, and motor skills. The midbrain enables auditory and visual processing, and the hindbrain facilitates involuntary (autonomic) functions like heart rate and respiration.[14]

Already you can see how these parts work together in a performance situation. The forebrain is engaged in interpretation, memory, and meaning; it also facilitates the physical playing of instruments (or acting, speaking, dancing, singing, etc.). The midbrain is involved in auditory and visual processing as we assess a performance in real time. Finally, the hindbrain is where performance anxiety comes in—pulse involuntarily quickens, hands become sweaty, and respiration increases.

## The Forebrain

The forebrain is the largest part of the brain, taking up well over half the brain's real estate. The cerebral cortex comprises the outer layer, which consists of the cerebral hemispheres. Both the right and left hemispheres can be further divided into four lobes: frontal, parietal, occipital, and temporal.[15]

A caveat: it's important to remember that our brains are complex mechanisms not entirely understood; even experts disagree on the divisions, labels, and functions of the portions of the brain. We're going to examine a few major players within the brain in order to understand the various roles they play in a performance situation, but it is likely that these different parts are even more interconnected than we currently realize.

### *The Frontal Lobe*

The frontal lobe is the largest of the four major lobes, located in the front of each cerebral hemisphere. It evokes creativity and allows us to assign meaning to experiences. The frontal lobe also assimilates personal values and aspirations, which then influence actions.[16]

I like to think of the frontal lobe as a former-hippie day care teacher swishing around in a colorful skirt that she sewed herself while on holiday at a yoga retreat. She believes we can do or create anything and urges us to find substantive meaning in it all. If we make a choice going against what we truly believe, she will shake her head sadly and wait for us to return to ourselves and our values. (For those of you who have seen *Bluey*, yes, I am thinking of a little Calypso romping around my frontal lobe.)

### *The Prefrontal Cortex*

Located on the most anterior portion of the frontal lobe, the prefrontal cortex is The Decider. It takes in information from the memory center, then processes all the old information and all the new information it can garner from the five senses.[17] Once the calculations have been made, it makes an informed decision. This is the part of the brain that engages when we think before we act.

The prefrontal cortex reminds me of the huge computer in *Willy Wonka and the Chocolate Factory* (the *real* one from 1971, starring the inimitable Gene Wilder), into which a scientist inputs gads of information in an attempt to locate the winning chocolate bars. Ideally, the prefrontal cortex spits out the right answer (hopefully more helpful than the movie computer's cheeky response).

### *The Motor Cortex*

Also part of the frontal lobe, the motor cortex is responsible for motor skills ranging from the gross motor skills we use every day, like walking and standing, to the fine motor skills we use as performers—playing a guitar or precisely manipulating the vocal cords to sing.[18] Gross motor skills involve the large muscles of the body, and fine motor skills employ the smaller muscles.

This part of the brain is like the innards of an old-school clock. It's the part that physically does the work—we can see the cogs moving together to enact motion, either on a large or small scale.

## The Midbrain

The midbrain is essentially a relay system that transmits information for seeing and hearing.[19] We utilize the midbrain when we practice and assess what we need to change about a performance based on what we hear or see. When we look into the audience and see facial expressions, or watch a conductor, we rely on the midbrain to channel that visual information. Likewise, when we hear the notes we play or sing during a performance, or listen to other actors for cues, it is the midbrain facilitating our audio processing.

## The Hindbrain

The hindbrain is responsible for autonomic responses like respiration, perspiration, heart rate, digestion, and so on.[20] These responses are involuntary, much to our dismay when we experience performance anxiety. The hindbrain simply wants the body to continue existing, so it regulates essential functions based on the information it receives. For instance, if it senses we're about to encounter a predator, it will slow digestion and redirect blood flow to other parts of the body most in need—the limbs, as we run away from the lion (or *elephant*). As we're running and require more oxygen, the hindbrain adjusts heart and respiration rates accordingly.

## The Limbic System

The limbic system is a complicated network of the brain involved with emotional and behavioral responses[21]—especially those required for survival. For our purposes, we will explore two very important components of this intricate web, both housed in the temporal lobe (See Figure 1.2).

### The Hippocampus

Embedded deep within the temporal lobe, the hippocampus can be considered the memory center.[22] It stores up all the things we've learned

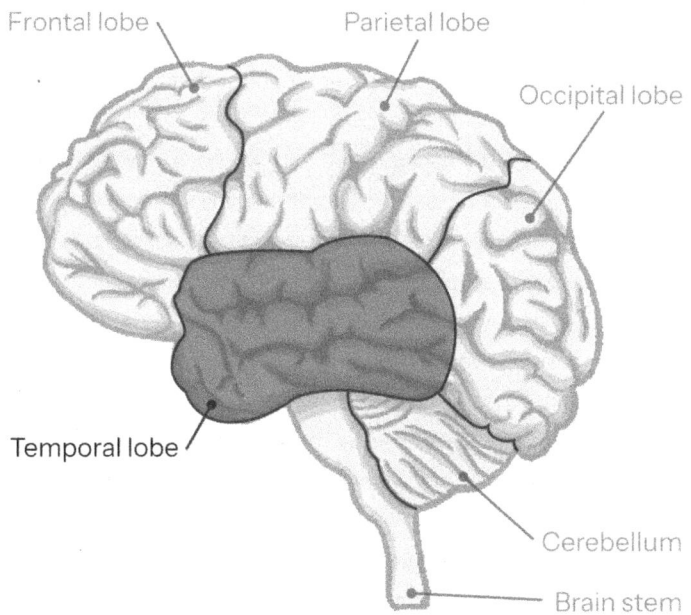

**Figure 1.2 Brain hemisphere divided into lobes.**

through practice and holds the important information until it is needed again. This could be the words to an aria, the outline for a presentation, or the plays for a sporting event.

If you've ever seen the Disney movie *Inside Out* (are you starting to piece together that I have small children?), you've seen the memory center in action. Important memories are gathered into crystal ball-like spheres that are categorized and retained until they're called up later. How about another children's movie analogy? Here we see Belle's massive library in the Beast's mansion; memories are crammed onto shelves like books, and we gaily soar along on a wheeled ladder, locating the exact memory we need.

## *The Amygdala*

Part of the forebrain, the amygdala is an almond-shaped structure housed in the temporal lobe. This little nut is responsible for everyone's favorite quick-fire responses of fight, flight, or freeze. It is also the major processing center for emotions and is responsible for linking emotions with memory.[23]

The amygdala is sometimes not-so-lovingly referred to as our "lizard brain." It's the part of our brain that evolutionarily kept our ancestors alive; it triggered running from the predator, fighting the predator, or playing dead so as not to engage with the predator. While we're running, fighting, or freezing, our body prioritizes survival and shuts down other functions that are unnecessary in our hyper-aroused state.

This chapter is called "The Problem," and we have now arrived at it. The almond-sized amygdala is to blame for the panic and anxiety that come flooding in when it registers a life-or-death situation (read: performance). I imagine the amygdala holding a tiny flag emblazoned with Taylor Swift's quippy earworm, declaring that it is, in fact, the problem. In reality, it's just trying to help you survive the lion. Interestingly, psychopaths have smaller amygdalae, causing them not to feel fear and anxiety. While it's tempting to envy their lack of anxiety, I daresay most of us would prefer to avoid the psychopath label, which arguably comes with its own problems.

As you can see, the brain is an incredibly complex and mysterious mechanism. The parts are so interrelated that we cannot simply say that *only* these segments of the brain operate behind the scenes of a performance. However, continuing with the backstage metaphor, it's important to know each stagehand's role and understand what happens when the stage director (the amygdala) loses its proverbial shit.

The brain is involved in a constant dance between voluntary and involuntary functions, choreographed by the parts we just examined. There are behaviors we choose to do, like walking onstage and opening our mouths to sing, which are voluntary. We make conscious choices to engage in those actions. Then, there are other things entirely outside of our control—the involuntary responses like heart rate, digestion, and so on, which go haywire when we experience performance anxiety. This involuntary system has two branches: the sympathetic and parasympathetic nervous systems.[24]

Performance anxiety results from an involuntary engagement of the sympathetic nervous system, though a systematic process:

- The body continuously takes in information from the five senses. This information is then processed through the various parts of the brain.
- The brain constantly scans the environment for danger. At some point, usually right before a performance or at a critical moment during the performance, it intuitively perceives a threat.
- The amygdala, sensing the threat, signals the adrenal glands to release adrenaline, fueling the fight-flight-freeze response.
- Involuntary processes respond to the threat, increasing heart rate, slowing digestion, redistributing blood flow, increasing respiration, and so on.
- The brain then stores the memory of the threat and response, so even once the adrenaline burns off and the anxiety fades, there is now another stored memory cataloging this particular threat.

## Adrenaline

We have all felt the rush of adrenaline, precipitated by a near crash on the highway, or a sudden slip on wet tile. It is a hormone secreted by the adrenal glands (hence the name) in times of stress. It is often an unwelcome guest for performers facing anxiety, but it does aid in heightening our senses and keeping us hyper-focused, which can be helpful in those same situations. For medical emergencies of extremely low blood pressure or cardiac arrest, adrenaline is a life-saving agent to quickly get the heart pumping again. You will recall that the amygdala is responsible for communicating with the adrenal glands, sending the message that we are in peril and need a sudden burst of adrenaline to fight, flee, or freeze.

Let's take a closer look at exactly how adrenaline causes the symptoms we feel when experiencing anxiety. We know adrenaline only impacts "cells that have adrenergic receptors; by sliding into these intricate structures like a key, adrenaline unlocks each receptor's capacity to set in motion cascades of signals."[25] *Cascades!* Yes, indeed, we are familiar with the *rush* of adrenaline—the *wave* of fear that comes sweeping in when we experience performance anxiety. The types of receptors in which adrenaline operates are alpha (alpha 1 and alpha 2) and beta-adrenergic receptors[26] (we'll get into those receptors more when we examine possible medications in Chapter 2).

Adrenaline impacts many systems of the body, which is why symptoms of performance anxiety are so varied among performers. Primarily affected is the cardiovascular system, as the heart beats faster and requires more oxygen for its efforts. Adrenaline also affects the musculoskeletal system, resulting in tremors, particularly in the hands. We also know it can have inordinate effects on muscular strength—it is how a panicking parent can lift a car to free a trapped child. Adrenaline can stimulate sweat glands, resulting in excess and immediate perspiration; or, it can affect the salivary glands, causing sudden dry mouth. It may impact tear production or cause dry eyes, or any number of other symptoms.

We must also consider noradrenaline (or norepinephrine), a chemical that acts both as a hormone and a neurotransmitter, working hand in hand with adrenaline.[27] A key question for me has always been: how (and more importantly, *when*) do adrenaline and noradrenaline burn out? We know that adrenaline surges cannot persist interminably, so what determines how long the anxiety attack lasts? These hormones are ultimately metabolized by two enzymes which transform them into inactive metabolites.[28] The sticky part of this equation is that these hormones and their effects can linger anywhere from twenty minutes to over an hour (exactly the length of most solo recitals and concerts!), depending on the trigger and whether the threat remains, either in reality or perception.[29]

In terms of performance anxiety, it is important to remember that our body physically responds the same way to all threats, whether that be an actual life-or-death situation, or the perceived threat of walking onstage for a performance. Our body senses the danger, sends a boost of adrenaline, and then expects us to start fighting for our life, running away, or freezing in complete and utter stillness. It does not understand when we respond by executing a challenging aria. It is our job as performers to assure the multiple impacted systems that we don't actually need the continual adrenaline dumping; we will not in fact die, no matter how bad the performance may be. That is the work we will undertake in the next several chapters.

## *Questions for Reflection*

- Create a timeline for your own performance anxiety. What do you notice first, and when? What happens next, and so forth? How long is the entire process of performance anxiety before your adrenaline "burns out"?
- What are your stored memories of performance anxiety? Do you have a prevailing memory taking center stage in your memory bank?
- What happens to you physically when you face performance anxiety? Catalog any somatic symptoms you've experienced.
- Think of the sensory cues you receive that trigger performance anxiety. What do you see or hear during or before a performance that contributes?
- What are some times outside of performing when you have experienced a rush of adrenaline? What were the sensory cues for those experiences? How did the physical sensations and/or timelines of anxiety differ in those?

## Notes

1. Cina, "Music Performance Anxiety and Cognitive-Behavioral Therapy," 53.
2. Cina, "Music Performance Anxiety and Cognitive-Behavioral Therapy," 54.
3. Cina, "Music Performance Anxiety and Cognitive-Behavioral Therapy," 54.

4   Dianna T. Kenny, "Negative Emotions in Music Making: Performance Anxiety," in *Handbook of Music and Emotion: Theory, Research, Applications*, ed. P. Juslin and J. Sloboda (Oxford: Oxford University Press, 2010), 433.

5   Gómez-López and Sánchez-Cabrero, "Current Trends in Music Performance Anxiety Intervention," 720.

6   Guillermo Dalia Crujdeta, *El Músico Adicto: La Musicorexia*. Madrid: IdeaMúsica, 2014.

7   Raúl Lledó-Valor, *Las Habilidades Interpretativas y Personales del Músico: Programa para Mejorar la Interpretación Saxofonística en Público*. PhD dissertation, Universidad Catolica de Murcia, Spain, 2022.

8   Jose Ballester-Martínez, *Un Estudio de la Ansiedad Escénica en los Músicos de los Conservatorios de la Región de Murcia*. PhD dissertation, Universidad de Murcia, Spain, 2015.

9   Ballester, *Un Estudio de la Ansiedad Escénica*; Lledó-Valor, *Las Habilidades Interpretativas y Personales del Músico*.

10  Cina, "Music Performance Anxiety and Cognitive-Behavioral Therapy," 57.

11  Cina, "Music Performance Anxiety and Cognitive-Behavioral Therapy," 56.

12  Ballester, *Un Estudio de la Ansiedad Escénica*; Lledó-Valor, *Las Habilidades Interpretativas y Personales del Músico*.

13  Dody Eid, "Divisions of the Brain: Forebrain, Midbrain, Hindbrain," *Simply Psychology*, January 17, 2024, https://www.simplypsychology.org/forebrain-midbrain-hindbrain.html (accessed March 15, 2025).

14  Eid, "Divisions of the Brain."

15  Eid, "Divisions of the Brain."

16  Cleveland Clinic, "Frontal Lobe," December 5, 2022, https://my.clevelandclinic.org/health/body/24501-frontal-lobe (accessed March 15, 2025).

17  Sandra Ackerman, *Discovering the Brain* (Washington, DC: National Academy Press, 1992), 65.

18  Olivia Guy-Evans, "Motor Cortex: Function and Location," *Simply Psychology*, September 21, 2023, https://www.simplypsychology.org/motor-cortex.html (accessed March 15, 2025).

19  Ackerman, *Discovering the Brain*, 16.

20  Ackerman, *Discovering the Brain*, 15.

21  Ackerman, *Discovering the Brain*, 21.

22  Cleveland Clinic, "Hippocampus," May 14, 2024, https://my.clevelandclinic.org/health/body/hippocampus (accessed March 15, 2025).

23  Cleveland Clinic, "Amygdala," April 11, 2023, https://my.clevelandclinic.org/health/body/24894-amygdala (accessed March 15, 2025).

24  Cleveland Clinic, "Autonomic Nervous System," June 15, 2022, https://my.clevelandclinic.org/health/body/23273-autonomic-nervous-system (accessed March 16, 2025).

25  Brian B. Hoffman, *Adrenaline* (Cambridge, MA: Harvard University Press, 2013), 124.

26  Hoffman, *Adrenaline*, 126.

27  Cleveland Clinic, "Norepinephrine (Noradrenaline)," May 17, 2022, https://my.clevelandclinic.org/health/articles/22610-norepinephrine-noradrenaline (accessed March 9, 2025).

28  Hoffman, *Adrenaline*, 124.

29  Cleveland Clinic, "What is the Flight, Fight, Freeze, or Fawn Response?" July 22, 2024, https://health.clevelandclinic.org/what-happens-to-your-body-during-the-fight-or-flight-response (accessed March 20, 2025).

# 2 Help
## *Medication, Therapy, and Other Options*

I am a professor, so I am naturally inclined to give homework, even to myself (hence the Questions for Reflection at the end of each chapter). I love reading. And yet, I have been disappointed at the end of every book I've ever read regarding performance anxiety because no book has uncovered the *source* of my own anxiety. Many of these books have titles with words like "conquer," "overcome," "fight," or "win"! To me, this has always rung false. I know in my bones that I can never truly *overcome* this thing. Believe me, I have fought that fight many, many times and never truly emerged feeling like a winner.

Many of these texts do include wonderful tools for tackling the *symptoms* of anxiety. Meditation, breathing exercises, visualization, and so on are extremely helpful. I admittedly do all of these things in practice and before every performance and recommend these steps for all performers (more on that in Chapter 10). Some books have powerful processes for performance preparation, like the five stages outlined in *Conquer Anxiety*.[1] Books like *The Inner Game of Music* helped immensely in my early performing career; I particularly resonated with some of the practical tips, like adopting a performing persona and dedicating pieces to particular loved ones.[2] Susan Stohrer gives excellent practical advice for performers of many types, including timelines for preparation, performance, and audition days.[3] Ultimately, I found these practices and techniques could only take me so far. And, I certainly didn't feel like I could claim to have *overcome* or *conquered* my performance anxiety at the end of the books, even having done all the quizzes and tried all the techniques (I am nothing if not a great student).

For me, performance anxiety has always felt more like a chronic disease than an acute ailment I could get over at some foreseeable point (like at the end of a book). My son's best friend has very serious asthma. He takes medication, keeps inhalers on hand, sees a specialist routinely, and tracks his oxygen levels regularly with an oximeter. He understands that he must relentlessly monitor this condition; when external factors change, he must be particularly vigilant in adapting and managing it. Barring an extraordinary medical advance in the future, he will never be considered "cured" or be able to proclaim that he has "won" this medical battle.

While I would prefer to be cured of performance anxiety, the idea of it as a chronic condition rings truer for me. I acknowledge there are things I must do to manage it as best I can, and I understand it will flare at times when conditions are right. I will keep monitoring and treating it, and using the tried-and-true methods that work for me at the time. However, I must remain ever vigilant and be willing to adjust my treatment accordingly. Furthermore, if we treat performance anxiety as a chronic condition, we must understand exactly what it's doing in (and to) our bodies, and what the root causes are—physical, mental, and emotional.

## Confession #1

I take a low-dose beta-blocker before important performances, and I see a therapist and journal regularly. I meditate (when I remember), and I exercise religiously. I keep trying to love yoga (I will never love yoga) and sit quietly with a cup of calming tea. These are the things that have actually helped my performance anxiety; the list is longer than I might like, and each of these things needs to be repeated over and over again. Unfortunately, there is no easy solution—addressing the root causes of anxiety requires a long-term investment in one's well-being. Your list may be even longer, and it may include different practices. The good news is that these things actually *do* help, and they come with a hefty bonus: this work impacts every aspect of one's life—relationships, self-worth, happiness, physical and mental health—while also minimizing performance anxiety.

Through the course of my research, I have come to believe that every theater, performing arts department, dance studio, sports team, and ensemble should employ an in-house therapist. I joke often, but I'm serious here. In the second season of *Ted Lasso*, psychologist Dr. Sharon Fieldstone arrives to help the team through a tragedy; this is the sort of sideline mental support I wish for performers. Imagine what we could accomplish if even a small percentage of the anxiety-riddled majority began to feel more empowered and could improve their performances even by a fraction of a percent. Imagine the varied world of performing artists we might have if those with high anxiety didn't quit the profession for something safer.

The medical community generally accepts that combining medication and therapy is the preferred and most effective approach for combating performance anxiety long-term.[4] I have found this to be true in my own experience. Since the number one question I receive from students is about medication, we'll start there.

## Pill Popping

Sometimes, when my children complain of a mysterious ailment or injury, I tell them I cannot help because I am not a doctor. They are quick to remind me that I am in fact a doctor, just not the helpful kind you'd want on a plane if something went wrong. I would like to remind you that I am not that kind of helpful doctor—and, even if I were, I would not be *your* doctor. We're about to talk about pharmaceutical intervention for performance anxiety, so I must interject here with a great big yield sign. PLEASE discuss your health and make any medical decisions, including medications, with a healthcare professional who knows your particular mental and physical health histories.

When I was an undergraduate, I wrote a paper on how *terrible* beta-blockers are for performers. I reported that they take away the edge we need while performing, and we simply can't anticipate how we will respond to them, so it's best to just stay safe. *Don't do drugs, kids!* Plus, who would want to listen to the lackluster performance of a glassy-eyed, drug-addled musician? *No, thank you!* I laughed nervously and looked around the room with wild eyes as I presented my paper, hoping someone—anyone—would jump in and refute my conclusions. I secretly chose that topic because I desperately wanted permission to try medication for my anxiety. I wanted my research to uncover a hall pass—the suggestion that maybe I could be saved, and maybe beta-blockers could be my golden ticket. To my great dismay, everyone in the class nodded in agreement: we wouldn't want to be *that* type of person who took pills for performance anxiety.

I understand that medication is a serious step and a decision not to be taken lightly. And yet, I have read in so many books and articles on performance anxiety, the same inferences that simply make my blood boil: *Take medication at your peril. Yes, it may help, but you really shouldn't. At all costs, don't lose that battle and give in to pharmaceuticals.* This sort of rhetoric furthers the shame we feel for experiencing anxiety in the first place. There is in fact medication that can mitigate certain somatic symptoms of performance anxiety. I cannot imagine a similar situation whereby we would discourage an asthmatic person from using their inhaler; even if the lung constriction was caused by anxiety, we would not begrudge them a few puffs to relieve the very real and dangerous physical symptoms.

I take beta-blockers before important performances. I have been taking them for over a decade, and I remain unashamed of my drug use. When my doctor prescribed them, he admitted that he took the same pills when performing in his barbershop quartet (an interesting fact to learn on the exam table). I learned that my minister takes these pills when she feels especially anxious before a sermon. I have since learned that many, many of my professional musician colleagues also take them pre-performance. Why don't we talk about it? Why do we discourage students from even thinking about starting this medication?

I have tried a few different kinds of beta-blockers, and I have settled on low-dose propranolol; I know the exact dosage I need for different types of performance situations. Propranolol is the most common beta-blocker prescribed for performance anxiety,[5] though there are others we will discuss. For me, the beta-blocker slows my heart rate just enough to keep the percolating in my chest at bay, and it prevents my hands from sweating. That's it. As a keyboardist, the hand sweating thing is huge. Not having to worry about slipping on the keys changed everything for me. Suddenly, the keyboard felt under my fingers the same way it felt in rehearsal, eliminating that particular source of anxiety.

Of course, I'm not suggesting that beta-blockers are right for everyone, or even most performers. For example, certain types can reduce saliva and dry out the mouth, so they can be detrimental for singers, actors, or instrumentalists like woodwind or brass players. Some people maintain a very low resting heart rate or blood pressure, and beta-blockers could be dangerous for them. Once, I had an incredibly stressful spate of concerts, rehearsals, and recordings that all piled up into one week. I typically only take beta-blockers a few times a month before very important events, so my body is not accustomed to prolonged use. In a spare hour between engagements, I ran to Target for some last-minute wrapping paper (because one must still play Santa for small children, even amidst holiday gigs), and as soon as I walked through the doors, I felt the edges of my vision blurring to black. I am a frequent fainter, so I knew what this meant. I took deep breaths and made my way to the restroom, where I sat in a stall with my head between my knees until I stopped shaking and could stand again. I stared at my pale face in the mirror and thought, à la the Berenstain Bears *Too Much Birthday*, "too much beta-blocking."

If you are looking for a hall pass and need someone to grant you permission to consider medication, here it is. You are an adult. You can make your own decisions, and only you know what is best for you as a performer. You are responsible for your actions, so be smart: consult your physician and monitor your response to any pharmaceuticals you take. There is a learning curve in determining your tolerance and the best dosage. Now that we've gotten the warning out of the way, let's examine how beta-blockers work and what the different options are.

## Beta-Blockers

Beta-adrenergic blocking agents minimize the physical symptoms of anxiety. As you notice from the long-form nomenclature, they work on the adrenaline that spikes with performance anxiety. As we learned in our discussion on adrenaline, that hormone can wreak significant havoc during performance. It can affect heart rate, perspiration, trembling, over- or under-salivation, digestive issues, and cause a host of other symptoms. Beta-blockers are designed to block some of these physical manifestations of anxiety, thereby interrupting the symptom-anxiety loop. When symptoms are blunted, people feel less anxious and think less anxious thoughts, which in turn results in less symptoms.[6] Performance anxiety and its symptoms create a vicious cycle, but beta-blockers can happily interrupt it (for some).

Beta-blockers have been prescribed since the 1960s for cardiovascular ailments. While there are many different types of beta-blockers approved by the Food and Drug Administration, propranolol is the most prescribed.[7] Others often prescribed for performance anxiety are atenolol, metoprolol, nadolol, and pindolol, each with varying levels of success in treating performance anxiety symptoms. These medications are either cardioselective or non-selective, which simply means they either target *only* the cardiovascular system (atenolol, for example), or they act more generally, targeting both types of beta receptors[8] (like propranolol). So, certain medications impact only heart rate, while others also mitigate additional symptoms (like sweaty hands).

Before we look at the specific types of beta-blockers and their efficacy for performers, let's look at who uses this type of medication. These statistics are from a very large study of over 2,000 professional musicians in the late 1980s conducted by Martin Fishbein and Susan Middlestadt. They undertook a national survey of forty-eight orchestras, including all major US cities. The results are incredibly interesting:[9]

- Twenty-seven percent of the musicians used beta-blockers.
    - Of those, 31 percent identified as female and 26 percent as male;
    - The most common age range for beta-blocker use was from under age thirty-five through forty-five.
- Of the beta-blocker users, 11 percent were occasional prescribed users.
- Of the beta-blocker users, 70 percent took them occasionally without a prescription.
- Very few reported usage before every performance (4 percent).
- Over 96 percent of users reported that beta-blockers were effective in reducing anxiety.

This seminal study also addressed common treatments for relieving performance anxiety:

- Prescribed medication was the top treatment among professional musicians (40 percent).
- Psychological counseling came in second, tried by 25 percent, and was ranked 60 percent effective.

- Other treatments included hypnosis (13 percent), yoga (9 percent), and massage (4 percent).
- The most effective treatment was rest, tried by only 3 percent, with a 100 percent success rate (!).

While this study is very interesting and provides helpful data, it is nonetheless nearly four decades old; many reading this book may not have been born when it was conducted. Anecdotally, I imagine the current usage of beta-blockers has skyrocketed.

In 2013, New York public radio station WQXR aired a piece titled "Musicians Use Beta Blockers as Performance-Enabling Drugs."[10] The piece begins:

> That age-old curse, stage fright, is nothing new. But for classical musicians it's come with a considerable stigma. Despite the fact that famous artists like Vladimir Horowitz, Renée Fleming, and Glenn Gould have all experienced crippling performance anxiety, a hush-hush attitude has prevailed.

Holly Mulcahy, concertmaster of the Chattanooga Symphony and Opera, is interviewed, along with other professional musicians who admit that beta-blockers are "in some backstage areas ... passed around like chewing gum or mints." Mulcahy recalls a time when a colleague ran around backstage frantically before a concert asking, "Oh my God, does anybody have any Inderal?"

Inderal is the brand name for propranolol, the most prescribed beta-blocker. Propranolol is non-selective, whereas atenolol and metoprolol are beta-1 selective and only target the cardiovascular system. The difference between selective and non-selective beta-blockers is important for musicians; you must inform your doctor exactly what you're required to do in a performance for them to determine the best drug for you. I am a keyboardist, so when I tried the atenolol a vocalist friend recommended, I found it reduced my heart rate, but it didn't do anything for my sweaty, shaky hands. When I went back to my barbershop-singing physician, he recommended propranolol, since it is non-selective and might help with more symptoms. Indeed, it not only calmed my racing heart but also kept the excess perspiration and tremors at bay. It *also* dried out my mouth, so while I could easily keep water nearby during my own performances, I understood why my vocalist friend opted for the atenolol instead.

Beta-blockers are game changers for many performers, though we must certainly consider a holistic approach to anxiety that goes beyond *just* medication. I love the story of Dr. James Black, the cardiovascular and gastrointestinal physiologist who invented beta-blockers. In 1988, Black shared half the Nobel Prize in Medicine for his work on developing beta receptor antagonists: "Upon learning that he had received the award, Black joked, 'I wish I had some of my beta-blockers handy.'"[11]

## Other Substances

Beta-blockers prescribed and monitored by physicians are generally well-tolerated with few side effects. The same cannot always be said for other substances desperate musicians may try. In the WQRX piece, Mulcahy relays that some of her music conservatory professors admitted to carrying around flasks of alcohol before performances. Indeed, even my own teachers laughed as they reminisced about taking a few swigs of liquor and performing under its influence in their younger days. Alcohol abuse is unfortunately common among professional performers, but most of us who have tried alcohol understand it is a risky option for musicians. Ethanol crosses the blood-brain barrier exceptionally easily and affects our senses, so it is dangerous to use for music performance anxiety. We need our brains firing at 100 percent in performance situations.

Some performers prefer natural remedies, and adaptogens have recently become very popular, especially for those who choose not to drink alcohol. Adaptogens are herbs, roots, and other plants with powerful stress-reducing properties. Reishi, cordyceps, lion's mane, and ashwagandha are adaptogens you may have heard of, which can ease anxiety and its symptoms. Adaptogens can be found in specialty non-alcoholic drinks, teas, gummies, powders, herbal supplements, and many other forms, which can easily be purchased online or in health food stores. Like propranolol, adaptogens are non-selective, so they can affect multiple symptoms of performance anxiety as they keep stress responses in check.[12]

Just because you can buy ashwagandha tea at Whole Foods doesn't necessarily mean you should brew without reservation. These herbs and supplements can interact with medications or exacerbate other medical conditions, so you still need to consult a doctor before taking them. For example, ashwagandha may interact with thyroid medication, causing it to be less effective. Additionally, supplements are not as highly regulated as pharmaceuticals, so you can't always be sure of potency, or even ingredients. Finally, it's important to remember that adaptogens (or even different brands or modalities) will affect each individual differently and may take effect within different timeframes. It may help one performer to sip ashwagandha tea right before an audition, but another may not feel the effects until later in the day, if at all.

In recent years, I have increasingly heard of students experimenting with cannabidiol (CBD). While CBD is not FDA-approved, it has been marketed for numerous health concerns. In a 2019 Gallup poll, 14 percent of Americans reported using CBD products; in 2020, as many as one-third of American adults reported using CBD.[13] In a 2023 bulletin, the Substance Abuse and Mental Health Services Administration advised that CBD products "are not FDA-approved, so despite being marketed extensively, there are no federal standards for their content, purity, or potency."[14]

Unlike other chemicals in cannabis, such as delta-9-tetrahydrocannabinol (THC), CBD does not alter the senses or cause psychosis or hallucinations. The short-term effects of CBD are quite varied, including changes in alertness, drowsiness, irritability, and agitation. It may also cause nausea or gastrointestinal distress, and it may interact with other medications.[15]

While beta-blockers work by blocking adrenaline, we're not quite sure how CBD works. It most likely impacts the cannabinoid receptors in the brain, which play a role in pain and anxiety. Anecdotally, students have reported that CBD is unpredictable for them—perhaps due to the lack of regulation in potency and purity. Some students report feeling drowsy or groggy when using CBD, and others feel it simply calms them down a bit. While CBD remains an interesting option for anxiety sufferers, it is likely not the best remedy for musicians, at least not currently.

There are, of course, other questionable remedies that musicians try. I have had students toss back melatonin gummies before a performance—melatonin binds to brain receptors to reduce nerve activity and induce sleepiness. It's safe to say melatonin is not the best bet for performers who need to remain alert and awake. Likewise, many of us may have heard the old advice to take aspirin and eat a banana before heading onstage. Bananas are high in B vitamins, which calm the nervous system, and they're a mild food that can help finicky stomachs. Aspirin and other nonsteroidal anti-inflammatory drugs can ease the symptoms of those who suffer from anxiety or depression related to brain inflammation. As with the other options outlined above, it is always best to consult your physician to see what may be safe and effective for you (except maybe the bananas—those are probably tame enough to try on your own).

## Therapy Options

My current therapist is an elegant, reserved woman who nods a lot and maintains an impressive poker face. She dresses impeccably and possesses the calm, self-assured demeanor I hope to achieve when I grow up. She is slightly older than me, but even if she were not, I think she would still exude the air of always being the adult in the room. I find her help invaluable. While I spent over three decades of my life certain I could do everything on my own and was not "one of those people" who needed therapy, it turns out that, in fact, I am. In reality, I think we all are. It is incredibly helpful to have a completely objective party—someone who is not, by default of friendship or bloodline, always on my side. From her bird's-eye view, she is able to see situations and relationships more clearly than I, and she affirms that my conflicted feelings toward my profession and performing are normal.

While I have become a wholehearted convert to this therapy thing, I realize it is a privilege. Therapy requires time, money, and (often) insurance benefits. Even when we possess those resources, it may take quite a long time to find a therapist who is the right fit. It is encouraging that especially since the Covid-19 pandemic, therapy options are more versatile and abundant. BetterHelp is just one online platform through which you can find a provider, have online or phone sessions, and even text your therapist between meetings, often without paying anything out of pocket after insurance.[16] Most campuses offer free student counseling services, and many insurance plans cover mental health visits to some extent.

The Covid-19 pandemic took a serious toll on everyone, and performers were dealt a specific sort of blow. We could no longer make music communally; concert halls and stages went dark. Many of us panicked about our finances—how can we make a living when workplaces are shut down? Some musicians worried they would lose the momentum of an established career—what if the Covid years were their best performing years, when they had just hit their stride or peak? Even more terrifying—what if we contracted Covid and it impacted our ability to perform permanently? Then, we must also take into account the technological advances that escalated during the aftermath of the pandemic. While it's heartwarming that an aunt from Kansas can watch a senior recital in Connecticut on live stream, it's also terrifying because that means *anyone* can watch the performance. Plus, these recordings often exist on the web forever, encapsulating both the good and the bad, frozen in time for unrestricted consumption.

One of the reasons I evaded therapy for so long is that I felt like I was *fine*, generally. Sure, I had some traumatic stuff in my past, but I was resilient, and I obviously survived. I had managed to be relatively successful at the things that really mattered to me, and I had built a (mostly) happy, healthy life for myself. *There are people out there who have it so much worse than me! THOSE are the people who need therapy.* Many therapists are quick to point out that we all suffer from the human condition; we all have traumas. People hurt us, and people abandon us, either by choice or circumstance. Relationships are complicated, and emotions are tricky. We all have coping mechanisms we can thank for getting us through hard times but may turn maladaptive. We have all suffered through the intense uncertainty of a pandemic, and if you've made it this far in this book, it's safe to say we all suffer from performance anxiety. The bottom line is that we can all benefit from an objective supporter who can help us see different angles and options.

## Cognitive Behavior Therapy

You may recall that the Fishbein and Middlestadt study ranked psychotherapy coming in second place among professional musicians, just behind medication as the mechanism they tried to alleviate performance anxiety. According to that study, 25 percent tried psychological counseling, and of those, 60 percent found it effective.[17] While beta-blockers can offer relief from some of the physical symptoms, they do not impact emotions or mental state. As performers suffer greatly from mental and emotional distress as a result of performance anxiety, treatment must be holistic, including approaches that deal with the performer's thoughts and emotions, in addition to the physical symptoms.

One popular mode of therapy is based on the interconnectedness of our thoughts, feelings, and behaviors. Cognitive-behavioral therapy (CBT) differs from psychoanalytic theory (think Freud), which suggests that our subconscious mind controls our thoughts, feelings, and behaviors. Instead, CBT is based on the idea that we can access and understand our own thoughts and thinking processes, and importantly, our thoughts can ultimately influence our emotions and behaviors.[18] Encouragingly, we are empowered to alter our thought processes and thereby alter our responses as well. A trained CBT clinician will use many strategies such as thought tracking, mental rehearsal, and exposure therapy to teach patients how to ultimately change their thoughts and behaviors.

In 2009, Deborah and Keith Dobson published the *Evidence-Based Practice of Cognitive-Behavioral Therapy*, bridging the gap between scholarly research and clinical practice. They posit that CBT has become a pillar within the field and is particularly poised to treat modern problems like anxiety disorders. One of the most common mental health disorders is generalized anxiety disorder, and CBT proves effective for anywhere from 38 percent to 63 percent of those patients. The Dobsons estimate that for most anxiety disorders, patients can be effectively treated with CBT in around eight to twelve sessions.[19] This is incredibly encouraging for performers who may have limited time or financial resources, as CBT is effective in a rather concise timeframe.

If you need further convincing that CBT is effective in treating performance anxiety, let's take a look at another study, this one from 1991 by Duncan Clark and Stewart Agras. In it, ninety-four musicians with performance anxiety were divided into three groups for treatment, which received:

1. CBT and placebo
2. CBT and beta-blocker
3. Beta-blocker alone

A control group received a placebo alone, and the study measured heart rate, self-assessment of musical performance quality, and subjective anxiety ratings. The authors noted that performance anxiety impacted their subjects to such an extent that the majority self-reported avoiding performance; and, similar to other studies we've examined, it suggested that most began suffering from performance anxiety as teenagers.[20] Clark and Agras posited that while it may stand to reason that performance anxiety could be mitigated by continued exposure, it is likely that negative associations with performing actually further perpetuate anxiety.[21] Their study ultimately found that participants who received CBT experienced less anxiety than those who received the placebo or medication alone. Interestingly, they also found the musical performances of these subjects improved.[22]

The data derived from this study is complicated; it is difficult to assign subjective numerical scores to musical performances. However, it is clear that CBT—either alone or in conjunction with medication—has a profound impact on improving performance anxiety, and may even improve the performance quality itself.

## Other Types of Therapy

If you've never explored therapy, you may not be familiar with the various forms. CBT is one specific type of therapy; it is focused on problem-solving and designed to provide specific tools for specific problems (performing). In contrast, other types of therapy are more generalized. For instance, often when we speak of "therapy," we refer to talk therapy or analytical therapy. In these sessions, the patient talks about any number of topics, and the therapist guides reflection by asking thoughtful questions and making suggestions. While talk therapy may also focus on problem-solving, its larger goal is understanding oneself, what makes them tick, and how they can improve any number of aspects of their life.

One specific form of CBT is cognitive processing therapy (CPT), which helps people understand and process their fears and traumas, ultimately reducing the pain associated with them.[23] This is an evidence-based, short-term treatment and is particularly effective in reducing symptoms of post-traumatic stress disorder. As such, it may be incredibly helpful for performers who have experienced significant or specific trauma.

Another specialized form of CBT is called acceptance and commitment therapy (ACT). While this field developed in the 1980s, it has recently gained increased traction within the psychotherapy sphere. ACT focuses specifically on mindfulness and acceptance of negative thoughts and emotions, such as low self-esteem and an inner critical voice.[24] It was invented by psychologist Steven C. Hayes specifically to address his own panic attacks and find effective treatment for other panic sufferers. Depending on geographic location, it may be challenging to find practitioners specializing in ACT, but it can be especially useful for performers with high anxiety.

Developed in the 1980s by psychologist Richard Schwartz, Internal Family Systems (IFS) views every person as a system of interrelated inner parts governed by a core Self. Through years as a family therapist, Schwartz discovered that many of these internal parts assume protective roles, shielding other wounded parts.[25] An IFS therapist helps people identify and assess their internal parts and the ways in which certain parts vie for control in various situations. This sort of therapy provides specific steps to control reactions and impulses,[26] and it may be particularly helpful for managing performance anxiety. In *Introduction to Internal Family Systems*, Schwartz reveals that he discovered a way to relate to his own anxiety, transforming anxiety-laden public speaking events into interesting challenges. Schwartz outlines the process of identifying the anxious part, being curious (rather than evading or challenging it), and finding the core traumatic experience fueling his anxiety.[27] Schwartz explains that he innately feels empathy and compassion for his internalized younger self, which remains scared of failure and ridicule; ultimately, his adult Self asks this protective part to step back, trusting the preparation that he has done. IFS may be a very valuable form of therapy for performers, particularly those who have experienced past traumatic performing experiences.

Another specialized form of therapy is eye movement desensitization and reprocessing (EMDR). This approach involves specific eye movements while mentally reliving a past traumatic event, with the eventual goal of reducing the vividness and emotional damage surrounding the event. If performance anxiety stems from a specific performing situation, or if a performer has suffered a major, specific trauma, EMDR may be helpful.

Another type of therapy you may have heard of is exposure therapy, and most therapists trained in CBT can guide clients through exposure work. For many years, this was considered the standard of care for people facing a fear. You can imagine people with arachnophobia visualizing a spider, then eventually looking at a (real) tiny spider in a jar, to perhaps taking off the lid, and maybe even approaching a larger spider over the course of treatment. In a similar vein, exposure therapy for musicians focuses on visualization of an anxiety-provoking event, then engaging in and surviving performance situations with various stake levels. You'll recall that in the Steptoe and Fidler study, music performance anxiety reduced with age, which initially led researchers to believe that repeated exposure led to a minimization of performance anxiety.[28] They later suggested that perhaps musicians with high anxiety quit the profession, but it is of course possible that exposure to performance situations does indeed lessen performance anxiety over the course of a career.

You may have heard of Toastmasters International, a group now over 100 years old. The group boasts over 270,000 members, with a goal of increasing public speaking skills through online and in-person meetings.[29] This is a sort of exposure therapy, and musical performance anxiety may similarly be mitigated by sheer number of positive exposures to performance events. Some researchers suggest that exposure therapy is most successful when combined with cognitive therapy, in which a therapist can assist the patient in reframing negative performance experiences into more positive ones.[30]

On the other side of the aisle, some researchers claim exposure therapy alone is not enough to minimize performance anxiety. As the Steptoe and Fidler study suggested, perhaps musicians facing high performance anxiety levels simply quit the profession, thereby skewing the results and causing the data to imply that exposure helps over time. Likewise, Clark and Agras undertook their study on CBT because they found that repeated exposure does not always result in lessened anxiety; in fact, recent studies suggest there is no concrete relationship between performance anxiety and age.[31] In a worst-case scenario, it is possible that exposure to performance without any therapeutic framing can worsen performance anxiety if one's thoughts and feelings about the performances are negative.

## Yoga and Meditative Practices

I don't like tea, and I don't like yoga. I have tried really, really hard to like both countless times, and I consider it almost a moral failing on my part to dislike these two things so severely. Nonetheless, no matter which yoga flow or room temperature I try, I simply do not enjoy it. Similarly, I completely concur with the fictional Ted Lasso's assessment of tea as garbage water. And yet, there is no doubt that tea is calming and yoga is therapeutic for both body and mind.

There is incredibly compelling literature on how yoga and meditation can actually rewire the brain; there are physical changes in the prefrontal cortex, hippocampus, amygdala, and other brain areas in people who practice regularly. Recently, studies have been conducted to see whether yoga can increase the efficacy of cancer treatments. Research proves that these practices result in relaxation, defined by a lowering of blood pressure and heart rate, and subjects reported feeling less stress.[32] As all these systems are impacted by performance anxiety, it stands to reason that yoga and meditation will help if we can dedicate ourselves to the practices.

There are any number of mindfulness and meditation practices that can help with anxiety. Apps like Calm, Mindfulness, and Headspace can provide guided meditations right at our fingertips. Meditation can be general focusing on breath and clearing of the mind, or it can have a specific purpose. The long-practiced "Inner Judge Meditation"[33] from Eloise Ristad's *A Soprano on Her Head* is a particularly helpful mental exercise for dealing with internal criticism. Ristad's book appeared in 1982 and was arguably one of the first texts to address performance anxiety and offer practical tips for addressing and mitigating it. I find particularly interesting her technique of trying to intensify one's symptoms—making our hands sweatier, or willing ourselves to become more nervous. This sort of brazen challenge often leads to a breaking point, almost miraculously causing the symptom to abate.

Many studies prove the efficacy of meditation; helpful for our purposes, one 2003 study dealt specifically with the impact of meditation on performance anxiety. Joanne Chang and her team examined performing students from several schools, including the Manhattan School of Music, Yale University School of Music, and others. They noted the incredible onus of performance anxiety on musicians and then suggested that while other practices like the

Alexander technique, biofeedback, exposure, and cognitive restructuring have all been tried and studied before, meditation had not yet been investigated as a tool for anxious musicians.

Their study involved a control group given no meditation sessions and a test group given eight weekly sessions of meditation training. All performers participated in a concert at the end of the eight weeks, and they were asked to rate their anxiety pre- and post-performance, as well as the extent to which their minds wandered and they experienced intrusive thoughts. Their findings support that meditation is a powerful tool in treating anxiety: compared to those who did not meditate before performance, a meditating group reported significantly less anxiety post-performance.[34] Meditation calms the nervous system, increases focus, and urges us to pay attention to our mind and body. It promises to have a positive impact on performance anxiety if we are able to dedicate ourselves to it regularly.

One meditative practice I find particularly helpful involves prayer beads, but anyone can adopt this practice even if they don't believe in prayer. I use a strand of prayer beads to go through the Biblical list known as the Fruits of the Spirit: love, joy, peace, patience, kindness, goodness, faithfulness, gentleness, and self-control. I work my way through the beads one at a time, thinking of a person, experience, or memory that brings up each particular idea for me. Sometimes I try to think of a musical piece or excerpt that reminds me of each virtue. This is a ritual I do right before I go onstage for a performance, often tucking the prayer beads into my pocket while I perform.

# Reading Fiction

When I was a senior in college, I grappled long and hard with what I wanted to specialize in during graduate school. I had double majored in music performance and English literature, and I had a considerably hard time with my Sophie's choice. In the end, I decided I would probably circle back to English eventually (after all, I wasn't sure I could tackle that pesky performance anxiety thing), but I should probably first go on in music, since kinesthetically it would be harder to take time away from my instrument and then resume after I'd attained an advanced degree in English. As you may have surmised, two and a half decades later, I am still in the throes of my first career—music. But, I have never lost my appetite for English literature.

If you have a hard time committing to a meditative practice, I have good news. In 2015, *New Yorker* magazine ran an article titled "Can Reading Make You Happier?" (Uh, yes!). The author cites a study showing that people who read a lot of fiction tend to be better at empathizing; we may even identify with characters and change our own selves for the better, based on what we perceive and believe about those characters. *Fiction can actually change lives.* Not only can reading fiction make us happier, but it can also serve a meditative function—it removes the reader from the present physical world. So, if you don't care to meditate, consider reading fiction instead. Similar to meditation, reading incites relaxation, resulting in lower levels of stress, improved sleep, lessened depression, and even higher levels of self-esteem.[35] Furthermore, reading fiction encourages visualization and imagination, which are especially helpful for performers. It improves focus, and readers typically have higher cognitive function than non-readers. Interestingly, there are actually even bibliotherapists who prescribe books as treatment! Reading fiction proves to be a powerful, and arguably underutilized, mental health tool.

## Sleep

The importance of adequate sleep cannot be overstated. I severely under-slept my way throughout all my student years. As an undergraduate, I was part of an honors college requiring us to submit weekly research papers at 8 A.M. every Saturday morning. I'm still unsure of the rationale behind that sadistic deadline; perhaps it was to keep us out of Friday night frat party trouble. The result was weekly all-nighters for nearly everyone in the program—particularly performing arts students who often had productions and concerts on Friday nights. Much later, my first child would sleep no longer than three hours at a time until he was over two years old; I know a thing or two about sleep deprivation. I will admit here that I used to think I was special. I actually believed that lack of sleep did not affect me. I wasn't so weak—so *basically human*—as my peers who gave in and went to bed instead of editing papers into the wee morning hours (spoiler alert: I was wrong).

While it is tempting to shirk sleep in favor of more practice or homework time, we do so to our own detriment. In a recent episode of his podcast *Huberman Lab*, Stanford neuroscientist and host Andrew Huberman stated that sleep is foundational for everything we do. He touts sleep as the very "bedrock" of our mental, physical, and emotional health.[36] In 2013, data showed that we have reached a veritable sleep crisis: compared to a century ago, people sleep on average 1.5 hours less per day.[37] We know inadequate sleep increases our risk for illness and disease, and drowsiness can be just as dangerous as drunkenness behind the wheel of a vehicle. Sleep deprivation has been used as torture, and a person will eventually die without sleep. In a 2013 study on adolescent students and sleep, researchers concluded that students who sacrifice sleep hours in order to study ultimately encounter more problems with tests and assignments the next day.[38]

As performers, our cognitive function must be at its very best. We execute technically demanding music, memorize entire scripts and librettos, learn staging and choreography for shows, use our voices and various other muscles to bring intricate scores to life, among other things. Our craft requires immense focus and the highest level of mental clarity. We cannot possibly make up for lack of sleep with medication, meditation, or anything else suggested in this book. Please, prioritize sleep, for your own sake.

## *Questions for Reflection*

- How do you experience anxiety? Does it manifest in racing thoughts, increased heartbeat, or flashbacks to past traumatic experiences?
- What things have you tried to minimize the symptoms of your performance anxiety?
- What has worked, and what has not?
- Have you considered medication? Would you try a selective or non-selective beta-blocker?
- What are some natural remedies you might try?
- Are there specific types of meditation or yoga that work well for you?
- Write a list of things you could work on with a therapist. This could include past traumas, relationships, performance anxiety, body image, and other issues.

- Ask at least five performers how they manage their anxiety. Inquire whether they are comfortable discussing medications, mindfulness practices, and/or therapy.

## Notes

1. Jon Skidmore, Rob Shallenberger, and Steven Shallenberger, *Conquer Anxiety* (Jon B. Skidmore, Steven R. Shallenberger, and Robert R. Shallenberger, 2020).
2. Barry Green and W. Timothy Gallwey, *The Inner Game of Music* (New York: Doubleday, 1986).
3. Sharon L. Stohrer, *The Empowered Performer* (Sharon L. Stohrer, 2022).
4. James A. Bourgeois, "The Management of Performance Anxiety with Beta-Adrenergic Blocking Agents," *Jefferson Journal of Psychiatry* 9, no. 2 (June 1991): 26.
5. Gertrude Parker Johnson and Brenda Crispell Johanson, "β Blockers," *The American Journal of Nursing* 83, no. 7 (July 1983): 1034.
6. Bourgeois, "The Management of Performance Anxiety with Beta-Adrenergic Blocking Agents," 16.
7. Johnson and Johanson, "β Blockers," 1034.
8. Cardiac and peripheral receptors.
9. Martin Fishbein and Susan E. Middlestadt, Victor Otttati, Susan Straus, and Alan Ellis, "Medical Problems Among ICSOM Musicians: Overview of a National Survey," *Medical Problems of Performing Artists* 3, no. 1 (March 1988): 4, 6.
10. Naomi Lewin, *Conducting Business*, "Musicians Use Beta Blockers as Performance-Enabling Drugs," WQXR, August 16, 2013, https://www.wqxr.org/story/3129230-muicians-use-beta-blockers-relieve-stage-fright/ (accessed March 1, 2024).
11. Hoffman, *Adrenaline*, 133.
12. Dana Ellis Hunnes, "What are Adaptogens and the Possible Benefits of Taking Them?," *UCLA Fielding School of Public Health*, February 16, 2022, https://www.uclahealth.org/news/what-are-adaptogens-and-should-you-be-taking-them (accessed February 24, 2024).

13  U.S. Congress, Substance Abuse and Mental Health Services Administration, *Cannabidiol (CBD) – Potential Harms, Side Effects and Unknowns*, February 2023, PEP22-06-04-003, Rockville.

14  Substance Abuse and Mental Health Services Administration, 1.

15  Substance Abuse and Mental Health Services Administration, 3.

16  betterhelp.com.

17  Fishbein et al., "Medical Problems Among ICSOM Musicians," 6.

18  Cina, "Music Performance Anxiety and Cognitive-Behavioral Therapy," 58–9.

19  Debora Dobson and Keith S. Dobson, *Evidence-Based Practice of Cognitive-Behavioral Therapy* (New York: Guilford Press, 2009), 183.

20  Duncan B. Clark and W. Stewart Agras, "The Assessment and Treatment of Performance Anxiety in Musicians," *The American Journal of Psychiatry* 148, no. 5 (May 1991): 604.

21  Clark and Agras, "The Assessment and Treatment of Performance Anxiety in Musicians," 599.

22  Clark and Agras, "The Assessment and Treatment of Performance Anxiety in Musicians," 602.

23  American Psychological Association, "Cognitive Processing Therapy," July 31, 2017, https://www.apa.org/ptsd-guideline/treatments/cognitive-processing-therapy (accessed March 19, 2025).

24  Cleveland Clinic, "Acceptance and Commitment Therapy," September 30, 2024, https://my.clevelandclinic.org/health/treatments/acceptance-and-commitment-therapy-act-therapy (accessed March 19 2025).

25  IFS Institute, "What is Internal Family Systems?" https://ifs-institute.com (accessed March 15, 2025).

26  Richard Schwartz, *Introduction to Internal Family Systems*, 2nd ed. (Boulder: Sounds True, 2023), 1.

27  Schwartz, *Introduction to Internal Family Systems*, 8.

28  Cina, "Music Performance Anxiety and Cognitive-Behavioral Therapy," 57.

29  Toastmasters International, https://www.toastmasters.org/about (accessed February 26, 2024).

30  Bourgeois, "The Management of Performance Anxiety with Beta-Adrenergic Blocking Agents," 25.

31  Clark and Agras, "The Assessment and Treatment of Performance Anxiety in Musicians," 599.

32  M. Alejandro Chaoul and Lorenzo Cohen, "Rethinking Yoga and the Application of Yoga in Modern Medicine," *CrossCurrents* 60, no. 2 (June 2010): 160.

33  Eloise Ristad, *A Soprano on Her Head* (Moad: Real People Press, 1982), 14–15.

34  Joanne C. Chang, Elizabeth Midlarsky, and Peter Lin, "Effects of Meditation on Music Performance Anxiety," *Medical Problems of Performing Artists* 18, no. 3 (September 2003): 128.

35  Ceridwen Dovey, "Can Reading Make You Happier?" *The New Yorker*, June 9, 2015, https://www.newyorker.com/culture/cultural-comment/can-reading-make-you-happier (accessed February 12, 2024).

36  Andrew Huberman, "Dr. Mark D'Esposito: How to Optimize Cognitive Function & Brain Health," episode 164, February 2, 2024, *Huberman Lab*, Scicomm Media, https://www.hubermanlab.com/episode/dr-mark-desposito-how-to-optimize-cognitive-function-brain-health (accessed February 26, 2024), 1:18:18.

37  Simon Williams, "Counting Sleep," *RSA Journal* 159, no. 5555 (2013): 36.

38  Cari Gillen-O'Neel, Virginia W. Huyna, and Andrew J. Fuligni, "To Study or Sleep? The Academic Cost of Extra Studying at the Expense of Sleep," *Child Development* 84, no. 1 (January–February 2013): 134.

# 3 Solid Ground
## *The Enneagram*

I've been seeing my massage therapist for nearly fifteen years; she was recommended by several colleagues who raved about her ability to keep them in peak performing shape. She practices and teaches "energy work," and I must admit that even a decade and a half later, I still have no clue what that means. Sometimes when I go in, she tells me one of my burners is low, or I'm harboring foreign energy. My eyes are always closed, so I really have no idea what she does about it, but I sense some waving of hands and special crystals being brought out. My mind doesn't understand her healing art, but my body does. I feel better when I leave her studio, and therefore I believe in it—or, at least, I believe in her.

We've already established that I am a skeptic by nature, but I realize there are things that I cannot fully comprehend that may have something to offer. One of those things for me has been the ancient wisdom of the enneagram. I have never really resonated with personality tests or typing, though I do find them interesting and wear my Leo and INFJ badges with pride. But, while listening to yet another podcast—Glennon Doyle's *We Can Do Hard Things*—I encountered the intriguing and life-changing work of Suzanne Stabile, the self-proclaimed Enneagram Godmother.

Here's where I will kindly ask the rest of you skeptics to retrieve your eyeballs from the back of your skulls and give this an honest shot. Whereas I have never learned much about myself from personality labels before, I have been amazed at the wisdom of the enneagram and how it offers continual work to do. For me, this has been the only real answer to my performance anxiety; it provides the solid ground I need in order to perform my best.

Let me first explain my journey in getting to this point. While I am naturally a pessimist, there are some hokey, rose-colored-glasses types of things I am willing to accept once I have experienced them firsthand. For example, I scoffed at the idea of love at first sight until I saw my future husband walking toward me and instantly knew with an epiphany-like surety that I would marry him and live happily ever after. (Now, to be fair, we met in college many years earlier, so technically this reunion wasn't *first* first sight, but the story is better if we just ignore that bit.) Likewise, I never really believed in light bulb-above-the-head *egads!* moments until I was walking my mini goldendoodle one February day and put together what I had learned from my recent study of the enneagram and my own experiences with performance anxiety.

I flashed back through my tenure of teaching performers, and it all seemed to click in an instant. The basic tenets of the enneagram aligned with my students' and my very different experiences with performance anxiety, boiling down to our different root emotions: fear, shame, or anger. I am part of the Shame Triad (classic enneagram type 3), so for me performance anxiety has always been about embarrassment, unworthiness, and the flashes of Imposter Syndrome that appear when I step onstage. But I have students who experience full-body panic—the traditional "stage fright"—and feel paralyzed by true fear when they perform. I have also had a handful of students who present as controlled and cool-headed, but whose jaws and chests tighten with anger as they fly into an internal rage—either at themselves, others, or external circumstances—when things go wrong in performance. Does one of these three types sound like you? I bet so.

The other part of enneagram wisdom that resonates with my experience is how we respond to the world, stress, and emotions: by thinking, feeling, and doing. For me, the best way to tackle my particular performance anxiety is through a combination of all three. I am disinclined to feel my feelings; I prefer to ignore them. So, for me, feeling the feelings actually seems like a threat to my life (cue adrenaline rush); I know I need to preemptively feel them so I'm not stuck in that fight-flight-freeze response onstage. It also helps me to engage in thought processes like the visualization exercises found in many resources on performance anxiety. The doing part is easiest for me. I've always been athletic, so I need to physically engage in movement to burn off some of the excess adrenaline. And, a physical task like running my fingers over prayer beads before a performance helps to ground me in the present moment.

We'll briefly examine the nine enneagram types in this chapter, but if you're interested in fully understanding your type and how it interacts with stress and in relationships, there are endless resources available to explore enneagram wisdom comprehensively. I would recommend taking an in-depth enneagram quiz, which you can do online, and listening to the podcast episodes of *We Can Do Hard Things* with Suzanne Stabile.[1] Do be aware that there are nuances to each type, and ways in which a number will pull to related numbers in times of stress or peace. Stabile's books explain all of these facets, and I cannot recommend them highly enough. In particular, *The Journey Toward Wholeness: Enneagram Wisdom for Stress, Balance, and Transformation*[2] is particularly helpful in addressing anxiety.

## The Enneagram

The Enneagram of Personality has been around for a long time, with parts of it harkening back to the ancient world.[3] Through continuous refinement, it eventually took shape as we now recognize it around the 1950s. The enneagram maps nine different personality types, sometimes called "enneatypes," and defines the basic characteristics, thought processes, fears, virtues, and traps of each type.

The nine personality types are:

1. The Reformer
2. The Helper
3. The Achiever
4. The Individualist
5. The Investigator
6. The Loyalist
7. The Enthusiast
8. The Challenger
9. The Peacemaker

Admittedly, it's challenging not just to choose the title we most want from this list (who doesn't want to be a Peacemaker?!). It's also difficult not to choose the label we've most often been assigned throughout our lives (e.g., many nurses are indeed Helpers, but profession doesn't determine type). Our true enneagram type is the one that gets at the heart of our *motivations*, not our behaviors. It's the way we view the world and how we are created by nature, rather than nurture. So, we must be careful to find the right categories for ourselves, while also realizing that we may overlap with other categories or may pull toward other numbers given our current circumstances.

The point of this book is not to determine your enneagram type—while there are some descriptors below, additional work may be required. I suggest taking an online quiz if you do not already know your type: enneagraminstitute.com offers the scientifically validated 144-question Riso-Hudson Enneagram Type Indicator (RHETI) for a nominal fee; enneagramuniverse.com provides a very accurate 180-question free quiz, which I often recommend to students. Once you have found your true enneagram type, it can be utilized as a tool for understanding your relationship with performing.

## The Enneagram Types

There are many effective ways to discuss the different enneagram types. It makes good sense to group the types together into their triads or stances in order to speak broadly about several different types at once. However, since I am a bit of a control freak, I am compelled to run down the list in numerical order; we'll contend with the groupings later. There are myriad books, articles, podcasts, and online resources covering enneatypes and their characteristics. Two seminal texts are *Understanding the Enneagram: The Practical Guide to Personality Types* (2000) and *Discovering Your Personality Type: The Essential Introduction to the Enneagram* (2003) by Don Richard Riso and Russ Hudson, creators of the Riso-Hudson Enneagram Type Indicator test. Much of the information below is distilled from The Enneagram Institute's online resources, and I would encourage consulting their website for more information.[4]

### *Type 1: The Reformer*

Reformers are natural perfectionists. They exude self-control and constantly assess situations, people, and themselves to effect meaningful change for improvement. This type is organized, prepared, and always informed; they often have very high standards. Such high standards can cause Reformers to be overly critical and impatient, and they can slip into perfectionism quite easily. Reformers fear being wrong or being exposed as defective in some way, and they often have very high moral standards and personal integrity. Ones are exceptionally successful and very driven, but they can possess a mean inner critic who judges and condemns everything they try to do as not being good enough. They are always striving to attain perfection.

## Type 2: The Helper

Helpers are genuine, empathetic people-pleasers. They possess true servant hearts and are excessively altruistic. Twos value being loved, and they constantly seek ways to help others, often from very pure desires to assist. Nurses and other compassionate professions are full of Helpers, who seek connection with others and find happiness in fulfilling others' needs. Twos have a hard time understanding that their help may not always be wanted or needed, and they sometimes impose assistance to the point of martyrdom, possessing a deep fear of being unneeded, unwanted, or unloved.

## Type 3: The Achiever

Many performers are Achievers. This type seems to excel at whatever they attempt; they are attractive, charming, and very driven to succeed. Achievers have seemingly endless energy to chase their dreams, and they often fixate on status and image. They have impressive credentials and will advertise their superiority; internally, once they have succeeded, they move on to conquering the next thing and have a hard time trusting previous successes. While they may exhibit the same perfectionist tendencies as Ones, Threes are often motivated by efficiency and goal completion, whereas Ones are motivated by a strong moral compass—Threes may even cut corners or cheat a little in order to reach their goals. Achievers fear being seen as worthless, and they strive to prove their worth, both to others and themselves.

## Type 4: The Individualist

Many artists are Fours. In an inner world of amazing beauty and drama, Individualists are often exceptionally creative and seek to share their internal experience with others through art. Many composers and singer-songwriters are Individualists; their deep emotional wells provide endless fodder for creative artistic endeavors. For Fours, ordinary life often isn't satisfying. They want the highs to be higher and the lows to be lower; they are typically in the throes of very big feelings. Fours want to express their individuality, and they fear not being significant in some unique way.

## Type 5: The Investigator

Investigators are eternally curious and questioning. They are often highly intelligent and innovative, coming up with novel solutions or ideas, and they can concentrate masterfully to hone specialized skills. Fives constantly learn and gather information because they fear being ignorant or useless. Investigators may spend so much time gathering information that they become scattered or paralyzed, and they may struggle to make decisions or take decisive action. Many inventors and innovators are Investigators. Interestingly, Fives are often unequivocally labeled as introverts, even when they are not. They enter each day with all the energy they will have for that day, and when it has been expended, they are entirely depleted.[5] So, of all the types, Investigators must ration their resources to ensure adequate energy for necessary activities and encounters.

## Type 6: The Loyalist

Sixes are hard-working, stable, and trustworthy. They strive for security and can be depended upon in any situation. Loyalists are excellent at spotting problems before they arise and swooping in to fix them collaboratively. They are group workers and will defend their communities or families at all costs. They are not unthinkingly loyal but will join a group of like-minded people and participate wholeheartedly for a cause they believe in. Loyalists want to be supported and to be in community, and their greatest fear is abandonment.

Sometimes, Loyalists can lack self-confidence or believe that they cannot face challenges on their own.

## Type 7: The Enthusiast

We arrive at the life of the party! Enthusiasts are just that—enthusiastic. They are gregarious, spontaneous, outgoing optimists. They are often entertainers, and comedy is a common outlet for this type. Always quick with a smile and able to make others laugh, Enthusiasts are versatile and up for anything. They can sometimes overreach their comfort zones, resulting in a scatteredness that makes them appear flaky or unfocused. While Enthusiasts are optimistic by nature, they can easily be distracted and can become burned out with their high-energy lives. Sevens fear feeling pain, and they may use cheerfulness and comedy as a crutch to avoid dissatisfaction or discontent.

## Type 8: The Challenger

Challengers exude self-assurance and strength, and they are confident in speaking their mind. Many Eights are business executives, favoring decisiveness and facing adversity head-on. They can use their incredible leadership abilities and strong will to make significant contributions within their circles, and they are often quite generous and inspirational. While Challengers are charismatic natural leaders, their strong personalities can also harbor hot tempers and mean streaks. They have more energy than any other type and are exceedingly capable and quick-thinking. Challengers can be confrontational in an effort to maintain their independence and control, and they fear being hurt or controlled by others.

## Type 9: The Peacemaker

Nines are laidback and easygoing. They naturally trust others and seek to keep peace and smooth over conflict. Peacemakers are inherently agreeable, which sometimes causes them to go along with others even when it conflicts with their own beliefs; they are able to see all sides of any situation. They are calm and open-minded, bringing others together peacefully, but they can also tend toward complacency or stubbornness. Peacemakers fear separation, and they most wish for inner peace and conflict-free stability.

---

Enneagram wisdom stresses that we cannot fully type others, since we do not know their innermost motivations. However, many public figures have written or spoken freely enough to give ample insight into their types. You can likely identify Robin Williams as a classic Enthusiast, Winston Churchill as a Challenger, and Mother Teresa as a Helper. We would categorize Mr. Rogers as a Peacemaker, Albert Einstein as an Investigator, and Joni Mitchell as an Individualist. Michelle Obama identifies as a Reformer, Ellen DeGeneres as a Loyalist, and Oprah Winfrey as an Achiever. You can probably identify the types of other public figures, and while personas can be deceptive, you probably know family members, close friends, and colleagues well enough to take educated guesses as to their types as well. As we'll discover in the next several chapters, learning about others through enneagram typing can result in richer, more empathetic, and healthier relationships.

There are further nuances (subtypes, for example) within the enneagram system that can offer additional insight into one's unique personality. Not everyone fits completely within these nine types; a person may mostly fit into one category but maintain a "wing" that overlaps with another. Additionally, all types pull toward another type during times of stress. While a person cannot essentially change types, it is possible for one's natural type to become obscured if their profession, upbringing, or culture forces habits or traditions that go against their true nature.

I began serious enneagram study several years ago when I stumbled across Suzanne Stabile's work. While I realized that I was a perfectionist long ago, I've always experienced guilt associated with this self-diagnosis. I could never shake my perfectionism, regardless of my intense efforts. Likewise, there were always parts of my closest friends and family members that I just couldn't seem to fully understand or access. For example, my daughter experiences emotions with a fiery passion that frankly intimidates me sometimes. On the other end of the spectrum, my son struggles to identify feelings and notices every small detail about his surroundings in a way that continually surprises me. Enneagram wisdom explains all of this and normalizes and validates our individual experiences, suggesting that the way we feel, act, and exist is the natural expression of our genetic makeup. It allows us to work on the weaknesses and further develop the immense strengths of our unique personalities. Furthermore, it encourages us to contemplate and appreciate the complexities of those around us.

For me, studying the enneagram has been incredibly fulfilling. I nearly sighed with relief when I found myself so clearly defined by it. I felt seen and understood, and I saw in it everyone I know. It taught me compassion for myself and others, and it encouraged the dominant parts of my personality that truly are strengths. But, moreover, it gave me continuous work to do to understand myself more fully and figure out how I thrive. This understanding in turn led me finally to grapple with my performance anxiety in a real way, rather than just treating the symptoms.

## Triads

The next three chapters address the emotional drivers for the three triads identified within the enneagram system:

- The Feeling (or Heart) Triad—Helpers, Achievers, and Individualists
- The Thinking (or Head) Triad—Investigators, Loyalists, and Enthusiasts
- The Doing (or Gut) Triad—Reformers, Challengers, and Peacemakers

Each triad is predisposed to an emotional reflex—a feeling to which they most reliably turn. Those in the Feeling Triad tend toward shame; the Thinking Triad most readily feels fear, and the Doing Triad is quick to experience anger. While it may be tempting to skip to the chapter specifically addressing your enneagram type, I would encourage you to at least skim the other chapters, as much of the information is universally applicable. For instance, most people experience Imposter Syndrome to some extent, which is covered in Chapter 4; Chapter 5 includes sections on risk-taking and combating fears, and Chapter 6 tackles self-blame. All of these topics are applicable to anyone experiencing performance anxiety. The next several chapters contain the bulk of our future work. So, take a deep breath, get ready to make some notes, and let's dive in.

## Questions for Reflection

- What enneagram type best fits your personality?
- Do you see ways in which your profession, circumstances, family, or culture have shaped your behaviors that may obscure or conflict with your natural type?
- What are the strengths of your type?
- What are the weaknesses, and where do you gravitate during times of stress?
- Can you identify the enneatypes of family or friends? How could this information enhance your relationships?
- How does this understanding of yourself and others lead to increased compassion?
- How does your personality type shape your experience with performance?

## Notes

1. Glennon Doyle, "Enneagram: Why You Are the Way You Are with Suzanne Stabile," and "Fix Your Most Important Relationships with the Enneagram: Suzanne Stabile," episode 226, July 10–11, 2023, *We Can Do Hard Things*, Audacy, https://momastery.com/blog/we-can-do-hard-things-ep-226/ https://momastery.com/blog/we-can-do-hard-things-ep-bonus-2/ (accessed February 20, 2024).
2. Suzanne Stabile, *The Journey Toward Wholeness: Enneagram Wisdom for Stress, Balance, and Transformation* (Westmont: InterVarsity Press, 2021).
3. The Enneagram Institute, "The Traditional Enneagram: Overview," https://www.enneagraminstitute.com/the-traditional-enneagram/ (accessed March 16, 2025).
4. enneagraminstitute.com.
5. *We Can Do Hard Things*, "Fix Your Most Important Relationships," 11:34.

# 4 Shame
## *The Feeling Triad (Helpers, Achievers, and Individualists)*

My daughter is probably an Individualist (type 4); she has always had larger-than-life emotions. I keenly remember the first time my very even-keeled son (type 5, most likely) experienced one of her epic temper tantrums. She was screaming to high heaven about butter (yes, butter—though honestly, SAME), red-faced and teary-eyed, spinning around and kicking her little feet on the hardwood floor of our kitchen. My son, who was born with the old soul of an eighty-year-old, looked at her, mouth agape, and said, "Mom. What on earth is she *doing*?" I laughed with him and replied, "Honey, she's feeling her feelings, and for her they are very, *very* big."

At six years old, she is endlessly creative and has verbal skills that are quite literally off the charts (recently she scored 197 on a test in which kids her age average twenty-five. I am bragging to further prove my Three-ness). She has the kindest heart, which is one of the things I love most about her. When we walk through the Middle Division playground to pick up my son after school, *everyone* waves hello and greets her by name; she receives hugs and high fives from kids twice her age. How do third graders know a kindergartener who doesn't even attend school in the same building? When asked, she says, "Oh, right! Once I gave that guy a pretty rock," or "That girl wanted one of my squeeze hugs!" She has recently begun to feel shame and guilt, which breaks my heart. These are feelings I know intimately, and I wouldn't wish them on anyone. She senses a miscalculation or infraction on her part, and she is immediately in tears: "Mommy, I feel like I did something wrong." Even if she did not, she cannot be convinced otherwise. I know she is cataloging these perceived sins internally so that she does not commit them again. I know this because it is what I have done my whole life. Welcome to the Shame Triad (also known as the Feeling Triad), types 2, 3, and 4.

# The Feeling Triad

Helpers, Achievers, and Individualists belong to the Feeling (or Heart) Triad; these types take in their environment and formulate responses based on how they feel. Members of this triad concern themselves so fiercely with what *may* happen that they often fail to appreciate or understand what *is* actually happening. They tirelessly seek the approval and love of others while struggling to believe they are actually capable of succeeding or being loved. Interestingly, the three types deal with feelings in very different ways: Helpers feel the feelings of others, Achievers try very hard to ignore feelings altogether, and Individualists internalize and amplify their feelings. They all belong to the Heart Triad, however, because of the way in which they naturally view the world—through the lens of feelings.

Helpers are naturally empathetic, assessing situations to determine how they can assist. This type exists entirely in relation to others. Twos ask others how they feel, and while they can express emotions, those emotions are usually those of others rather than their own. Helpers are exceptionally altruistic, but they often secretly expect something in return, so they become frustrated or hurt when they've given so much of themselves and feel underappreciated or taken for granted. This type often has very few boundaries, giving selflessly to the point of exhaustion. I'm reminded of the children's book *The Giving Tree* when I think of Twos. In it, Shel Silverstein writes of an apple tree that loves a little boy dearly. The tree happily gives its apples, shade, bark, and wood, until finally, it is a decimated stump.[1]

Achievers are incredibly high-energy, busy, competitive people. They often devote themselves entirely to work, relationships, hobbies, and literally any other task to keep themselves from feeling emotions (usually subconsciously); these qualities are often highly valued within American working culture. Interestingly, while Achievers take in the world through feeling, they then readily ignore that information or repress the feelings that arise. They often play many roles, becoming whoever they need to fit a certain situation or relationship. Continuing with the children's book theme, Threes are *The Little Engine That Could*, never giving up and doggedly working toward their goals: *I think I can, I think I can, I think I can.* . . . Like the little engine, they typically succeed to much acclaim.

Individualists are incredibly complicated folks. This type seeks beauty and drama, and when they cannot find it, they create it themselves, often unintentionally. Stabile notes that Fours are comfortable with melancholy, but our culture often mistrusts or disallows such wallowing in dark emotions.[2] Relationships are incredibly important to Individualists, but for fear of being disappointed or rejected, they often look for mistakes or flaws in others. Fours are exceptionally afraid of being abandoned, and they can sometimes self-sabotage or take on more than they can handle. Here I'm going to jump literary categories and consider the complex novel *Life of Pi*. The main character develops a brilliant, wildly dramatic world of his own imagination in order to explain a profound trauma to himself and others. Like Fours, the narrator sees the world in brilliant technicolor, where both joy and sorrow are all-encompassing.

The three types contained in this triad utilize feelings in very different ways, but they nonetheless view the world through the filter of their hearts. Helpers, Achievers, and Individualists create immense beauty, attend to the emotions of others, and enable families, corporations, and entire industries to thrive. Their downfall is that they often lose sight of themselves in their efforts to identify and empathize with the feelings of others. In caring for others' emotions, these types often lose sense of who they truly are, tending toward shame so fiercely that it can actually subsume their identities.[3] Here we arrive at the crux of the issue for the Feeling Triad: shame. It is, I believe, for Helpers, Achievers, and Individualists, the fuel that drives and accelerates performance anxiety.

## Shame

We probably all have our own definitions of shame and can locate exactly where this feeling manifests in our bodies. For me, it is a sort of sinking feeling, a nauseating weight pressing down from my chest to my belly. My ears burn, my saliva flows, and my jaw tightens. I imagine that my insides are boiling into an oozing, lava-like ore. This is accompanied by the deep sense that I am innately, irrevocably flawed. Acclaimed author and shame researcher Brené Brown defines, "Shame is the intensely painful feeling or experience of believing we are flawed and therefore unworthy of acceptance and belonging."[4]

Shame is a tricky feeling, and it is easily mistaken for other feelings like embarrassment, humiliation, or guilt. Importantly, while both guilt and shame are products of self-critique, shame internalizes badness as a part of one's identity, whereas guilt underscores that a person has *done* something bad.[5] It is important to note that anyone can feel shame and guilt, not just those in the Feeling Triad. However, shame is the dominant feeling toward which enneagram types 2, 3, and 4 tend.

Brown suggests that shame is fueled by a fear of losing connection with others. Helpers, Achievers, and Individualists fear what others think, assuming that they are bad if others criticize or ridicule them—members of the Feeling Triad are unable to separate performance from person. If others see them as the flawed beings they know they are, certainly everyone will abandon them, rightfully deeming them unworthy of love and acceptance. Those in the Feeling Triad simply cannot risk being proven right about their unworthiness.

## Shame and Anxiety

For Helpers, Achievers, and Individualists, shame and anxiety lurk around every corner, waiting for any opportunity to spring out of the shadows. Stabile suggests that this triad could just as easily be referred to as the "anxiety triad," because they are constantly anxious about all aspects of their lives, performance, and relationships. In fact, these types often confuse or even transmute other emotions into anxiety.[6] The Feeling Triad is arguably the most anxious triad, and Twos, Threes, and Fours can often identify and explain their own anxiety expertly. Many members of this triad suffer from generalized anxiety or report experiencing some level of anxiousness in everyday life.

Many, many performers belong to the Feeling Triad. Achievers enjoy the spotlight and often believe their worthiness is tied to onstage successes. Individualists are exceptionally creative types, and singer-songwriters, composers, and directors frequently belong to this type. While Helpers may make up a smaller percentage of performers, these folks are often the overworked and underappreciated performers who assist everyone else in addition to carrying out their own performance goals. Since this triad is linked so intrinsically with anxiety, often even turning other emotions *into* anxiety, performers in this triad are particularly susceptible to performance anxiety.

Dr. Dianna Kenny, who provided the comprehensive definition of music performance anxiety in the first chapter, published the groundbreaking textbook *The Psychology of Music Performance Anxiety* in 2011. As a psychologist, Kenny discusses the phenomenology and epidemiology of music performance anxiety and covers several different theories of anxiety before addressing comprehensive treatment options and ways to prevent it. Kenny proposes three different types of performance anxiety: the first is focal, in which a performer experiences focused anxiety surrounding a particular type of performance (like an audition). The second is a more generalized anxiety disorder, in which a performer also suffers from social anxiety separate from performing. For our purposes in this chapter, I am most interested in her third category, in which performance anxiety manifests in response to a conditional sense of self-worth, which often develops early in life. This group experiences such overwhelming anxiety that they begin to associate it with their very identities.[7]

Kenny suggests that performers suffering from this very high level of anxiety equate successful performance with their own self-worth, therefore placing exorbitant amounts of pressure on themselves to perform well. Unlinking performance from self-worth may seem like a never-ending battle. Kenny suggests that this personality trait is often developed very early in life, and these early experiences of low self-worth negatively affect and influence behavior, relationships, and emotional health throughout life.[8]

Severe performance anxiety is multifaceted and often stems from past life experiences beyond our control; the only way to peel back the layers of this particularly tear-inducing proverbial onion is through intentional—and often painful—self-work. A trained therapist can help, as can honest journaling or frank conversations with close friends. Performers from the Feeling Triad are particularly susceptible to shame, which is an exceptionally powerful driver: shame can generate exponential amounts of anxiety. If these performers additionally belong to the severe-anxiety subset Kenny suggests, shame and anxiety can collude, proving utterly crippling in performance situations.

# Imposter Syndrome

Performers with high anxiety and shame often fall victim to what is known as Imposter Syndrome. I described a situation in the Prologue in which I felt like a foolish poseur, lecturing a group of musicians on performance anxiety after I had just succumbed to its pressures in a recital. This is the gist of Imposter Syndrome, which is not actually a "syndrome," as the thoughts and feelings of unworthiness only appear at certain times, rather than continuously. In 1978, clinical psychologists Clance and Imes discovered that their female students were particularly predisposed to doubting themselves and their achievements (Imagine that! See Chapter 9 and the section on "Gender" for more on this topic). After 150 interviews, Clance and Imes coined the term "imposter phenomenon," which suggests an internal experience of self-doubt in which people believe they are not as intelligent as their academic records may suggest, and that they have somehow tricked others into believing they are smart and worthy of success.[9]

Nearly 70 percent of people have felt Imposter Syndrome to varying extents,[10] so it is not entirely confined to this triad. But, studies prove that those who are predisposed to anxiety and perfectionism are also more likely to experience imposter fears.[11] The hits just keep on coming! Not only are Helpers, Achievers, and Individualists more likely to experience anxiety and shame, but they are also more likely to suffer from Imposter Syndrome-not-syndrome. It seems an unbearable, unbreakable loop—shame fuels anxiety, which in turn fuels imposter fears. Repeat, repeat, repeat.

So, what can be done about Imposter Syndrome? Simply put, performers must trust past experiences, utilizing previous success as factual data that implies future success. This may seem overly simplistic, but it is hard-won for members of the Feeling Triad: *trust the data*. This triad inherently views life through the lens of the heart and feelings, but in order to amass, analyze, and utilize data, members of the Feeling Triad must employ their *minds* (which is more in the Thinking Triad's wheelhouse). For the Feeling Triad, data is somewhat unreliable: while they may acknowledge and even believe it, they do not *trust* it. Helpers, Achievers, and Individualists must take the data at face value and use it to dismantle any beliefs to the contrary. Those living in the Feeling Triad have a very hard time believing that success is not simply a fluke or result of their cunning or trickery. To counter this, they must do the hard work of proving themselves wrong: they must document the actual evidence, proving to themselves that their successes are valid and honestly achieved.[12] The good news is that we possess all of this data; we don't need to do external research to accumulate these statistics. By listing all past successes, we can create a data set that contradicts *feelings*, which are frankly unreliable.

Feeling Triad types must also remember that criticism does not equate to failure. People will formulate opinions about us, our appearance, our actions, our performance, and any number of other things. Performers are particularly susceptible to adjudication and frequently in the public eye. When receiving criticism, Helpers, Achievers, and Individualists accept those critiques as judgment on their *character*, rather than commentary on their *performance*. This, of course, goes hand in hand with Brown's distinction between shame and guilt—shame tells us *we* are bad; guilt tells us our *behavior* was bad. Those in the Feeling Triad tend to internalize criticism as an attack on themselves, proof that *they* are bad, rather than assessing criticism in relation to specific events or actions, external to their being.

## Confession #2

I used to lie a lot. This is not necessarily pride-inducing, but as a Three with a self-preservation subtype, it is not all that surprising. Through a lot of therapy, I've learned that I lie in order to maintain the illusion of control. If I don't tell you the truth about what I've had for lunch, in my messed-up way of thinking, I keep the upper hand by knowing something that you don't know. Throughout my early life, I possessed very few scruples about lying. I would mostly lie about small things to keep myself out of trouble, but over time I also lied about some rather important things, to some rather important people. And then, I met my future husband (a Five), who does not lie. Untruthfulness confuses him. I have found that the amount I lie is in direct correlation to how much I like and respect a person; I have lied less to my husband than to anyone else in my entire life, and that is the biggest compliment I can give.

Lying is how I know that I am an Achiever and not a Reformer (Ones have an exceptionally strong moral compass). I always assumed that *everyone* was lying most of the time. It turns out that's not true (see, I can lie even to myself!). In her painfully honest memoir on sobriety, *We Are the Luckiest,* Laura McKowen dedicates an entire chapter to her untruthfulness:

> I hadn't noticed it happening. There was no decision or abrupt change in direction: *Now I am going to lie.* It was a gradual turning away and shrinking: a small twist of words here, a detail left out there, a matter of fractions of millimeters at a time, and suddenly I found myself boxed into a very small room.[13]

Like McKowen, I finally realized that lying is a convoluted way of trying to preempt shame, though usually ineffective. If we are petrified of exposing our vulnerabilities, we will construct elaborate lies to keep others at arm's length. We will even lie about small things, deceiving even those who want to help us—like therapists and spouses. Perhaps you've also done this: someone asks if you've heard of an author or seen a classic movie, and instead of admitting that you have not, suddenly a little white lie pops out and you feign understanding. Truthfulness makes us vulnerable, and those in the Shame Triad struggle to believe they are loveable and worthy as they are, without the facade and glossy shine of their lies. McKowen suggests responsibility as the healthy alternative to lying—assuming accountability for every aspect of your life.[14] As part of my self-learning journey, I have sought to take responsibility for everything that happens to me and everything I say and do, both to others and myself. To that end, I promise that everything I have written in this book is true. (Mostly.)

Telling and trusting the truth is part of the hard work Helpers, Achievers, and Individualists must do to tackle shame, perfectionism, Imposter Syndrome, *and* performance anxiety. Telling the truth necessitates vulnerability; it takes courage: "*Courage* is a heart word. The root of the word *courage* is *cor*—the Latin word for heart. In one of its earliest forms, the word *courage* meant 'To speak one's mind by telling all one's heart.'"[15] Uncovering the truth can be challenging for those in the Feeling Triad—they often obscure the truth by heaping shame and anxiety into mountains so high that the truth can no longer be found.

## The Work

Those in the Feeling/Shame Triad have a lot of work to do and have already received several important assignments: identify and trust the data, work to apply criticism to performance rather than personhood, uncover, tell, and believe the truth, and identify shame and anxiety when they occur, ascertaining their true cause. This probably seems like enough to occupy Helpers, Achievers, and Individualists for a lifetime, but there is yet more necessary work to fully understand yourself and your unique, complex brand of performance anxiety.

First, Helpers, Achievers, and Individualists must tackle shame. It is the root cause of a great deal of anxiety among members of the Feeling Triad. Brené Brown writes that while no one can become *resistant* to shame, we can become *resilient* in the face of it, identifying shame when it appears and learning from those experiences. She writes, "By *resilience*, I mean that ability to recognize shame when we experience it, and move through it in a constructive way that allows us to maintain our authenticity and grow from our experiences."[16] Brown suggests that on the opposite end of the continuum from shame is empathy. Members of this triad must work to cultivate empathy, both for themselves and others. Engaging in empathy, directed both internally and externally, is the only lasting way to combat shame. Simply put: cut yourself some slack.

In order to identify shame and cultivate empathy, we must also be willing to seek, tell, and trust the truth. This can be particularly challenging for members of the Feeling Triad (but then, no one promised this work would be easy). In addition to taking responsibility for actions, members of this triad must also gather objective data and trust the results. When you list your successes, what does the data prove? Are you willing to trust it?

For me, one of the most compelling aspects of the enneagram is the rich body of work it engenders and requires. We could engage in this work endlessly, and it is specific to our types. Stabile suggests that members of the Feeling Triad must work toward loving themselves for who they truly are, rather than loving their image or their many important roles.[17] This may sound like infuriatingly vague advice. *How the hell am I just supposed to start LOVING myself?* I will gently argue that you are already making headway. You picked up this book and are about halfway through it; engaging meaningfully in self-reflection and discovery is an act of self-love. You recognize that performance anxiety is a serious struggle, and you have mustered enough self-compassion to do something about it.

Here is some additional work for each specific type, which may be best explored in a journal dedicated to better understanding your performance anxiety:

## Type 2: Helpers

- Realize when you are helping just to please. Try to be honest in your motivation for assisting and caring for others.
- Exercise your right to say "no" in situations when your motivation to help isn't clear or honest.
- Create boundaries to define what you are freely willing to do for others and what you are unwilling to do.
- Understand that you cannot care for others without first caring for yourself. Invest in yourself, regularly setting aside time for self-care.
- Note the way others demonstrate care and affection, which may be different from yours. Remember that they cannot read your mind to know how you would like to be treated.
- Recognize when you are burnt out, overwhelmed, or resentful as a result of caring for others, and rest in response.
- Believe that you are loved and worthy for who you are, not what you do.
- Cultivate the relationships you already have, and carefully examine the costs of new relationships before committing to them.
- Notice when you feel responsible for saving others, and remember that everyone is responsible for their own feelings and actions.
- Know that you do not need to win others' affection by doing things for them.

## Type 3: Achievers

- Know that your worth is not dependent on your success.
- Realize that you cannot make everyone like you, and you will exhaust yourself if you try.

- Notice when you are blindly chasing goals and doing whatever it takes to achieve them. Are you still caring for yourself and others in the process?
- Determine what your genuine goals and motivations are. What truly makes you happy? Try to follow those aspirations rather than what you believe others expect.
- Prioritize your energy and time. What is worth your entire effort, and what can be done with less effort?
- Identify what you are feeling as you feel it. Journal or talk with a therapist or friend about your emotions, realizing that ignoring them will cause bigger problems in the end.
- Notice when you feel competitive toward others, remembering that there is room for everyone to succeed.
- Acknowledge when you have fully completed a task, rather than believing there is always something more you should do.
- Invest in relationships, knowing that others appreciate who you are, not only what you have accomplished.

## Type 4: Individualists

- Engage in artistic and creative endeavors that energize you, even if you do not excel at them.
- Notice when you tend toward emotional extremes, and ask whether the situation warrants heightened emotion.
- Identify actions to take when you experience sadness or melancholy. Make a list of things that uplift your spirit, such as taking a walk or listening to music.
- Know that you are loved and seen exactly as you are—you do not need to change aspects of yourself for others.
- Make a list of your good qualities and refer to it often.
- Understand that your imagination is powerful; commit to living in the present reality rather than fantasizing about the future or ruminating on the past.

- Recognize your tendency to pull away from others when they disappoint or anger you; try not to compare yourself to others.
- Acknowledge and appreciate the many mundane, average parts of life and know that they are equally important and valuable. Attempt to find beauty in stability rather than actively seeking extremes.

Members of the Feeling Triad are particularly susceptible to feelings of shame and anxiety. While I am a strong believer that *everyone* can benefit from psychotherapy, Helpers, Achievers, and Individualists may be particularly helped by this intervention and may also benefit greatly from mindfulness practices like meditation, yoga, journaling, or reading fiction (these practices are addressed in Chapter 8). Additionally, since members of this triad are prone to higher levels of anxiety, these types might consider discussing medication with a doctor. *Please remember that I am not a medical doctor, and anxiety medication is not right for everyone.* However, I do believe strongly that those who suffer from high levels of performance anxiety might be helped by pharmaceutical intervention. Most importantly, we need to do this work, and do it honestly.

## *Questions for Reflection*

- How does shame feel in your body? When do you experience it?
- Make a list of times when you have felt shame. Was it accompanied by anxiety?
- What have you read about your enneagram type that feels true to you? What does not?
- Have you suffered from Imposter Syndrome? What were the conditions under which it occurred?
- Make a comprehensive list of the objective data: your successes and failures. What does the data prove about your worthiness or ability?
- What are some exercises you can adopt for your specific enneagram type?
- Do you believe shame may be the driver of your performance anxiety? Why or why not?

# Notes

1. There is a redeeming, hopeful ending in which the boy, now an elderly man, returns to the tree asking only for a place to rest. The stump provides this, satisfied to once again be with the beloved boy.
2. Stabile, *Journey*, 56.
3. Stabile, *Journey*, 35.
4. Brené Brown, *I Thought it was Just Me (But it Isn't): Making the Journey from "What Will People Think" to "I Am Enough"* (New York: Avery, 2007), 5.
5. Brown, *I Thought*, 13.
6. Stabile, *Journey*, 35.
7. Dianna T. Kenny, *The Psychology of Music Performance Anxiety* (Oxford: Oxford University Press, 2011), 233.
8. Kenny, *The Psychology*, 233–5.
9. P. R. Clance and S. A. Imes, "The Imposter Phenomenon in High Achieving Women: Dynamics and Therapeutic Intervention," *Psychotherapy: Theory, Research, and Practice* 15, no. 3 (1987): 241.
10. Jessamy Hibberd, *The Imposter Cure: How to Stop Feeling Like a Fraud and Escape the Mind-Trap of Imposter Syndrome* (London: Aster, 2019), 30.
11. Hibberd, *The Imposter Cure*, 61.
12. Hibberd, *The Imposter Cure*, 85.
13. Laura McKowen, *We Are the Luckiest: The Surprising Magic of a Sober Life* (Novato: New World Library, 2020), 154.
14. McKowen, *We Are the Luckiest*, 177.
15. Brown, *I Thought*, xxiii.
16. Brown, *I Thought*, 31.
17. Stabile, *Journey*, 36–7.

# 5  Fear
## *The Thinking Triad (Investigators, Loyalists, and Enthusiasts)*

I do not often experience fear. In our household, I am the one who deals with spiders, and if our home alarm faults in the middle of the night, I jump out of bed and race around the house searching for intruders (weaponless and sightless, sans contacts). When I was thirty-three weeks pregnant with my son, I went to the hospital for an ultrasound and fetal non-stress test, which I was required to have twice a week due to my worsening preeclampsia symptoms and his refusal to grow in utero. The ultrasound technician grew visibly alarmed when she could not locate his heartbeat. She turned me on my side, gave me orange juice, and finally used an electric prod in futile attempts to encourage him to move. Her movements got quicker and her face more drawn as she typed furiously. I watched her shoulders rise and her breathing quicken, and I knew we were in trouble. Indeed, there was insufficient amniotic fluid, and despite all efforts, she could not locate his heartbeat.

Once I was quickly admitted to the hospital—without the "go bag" that I had not yet prepared seven weeks early, or a car seat properly installed in my waiting vehicle—my doctor found a weak heartbeat, and I lay on my left side desperately trying to reach my husband, who was in another state for work. My medical team induced preterm labor, and in a scene straight out of *Home Alone*, my poor husband ran from airline to airline, begging to get home, at whatever cost. (He later told me that he would never reveal just how much he ended up spending on that ticket, and indeed, he hasn't.) Since labor ended up lasting over seventy-two hours, he made it with time to spare. When my son was *finally* born, he was blue and unbreathing. I watched my obstetrician's grim face and saw six NICU nurses working frantically on my tiny son. No one would—or could—answer my repeated cries: *Is he OK? Will he be OK? Tell me if he's OK*. Or, maybe I was too terrified to speak the questions aloud.

He was OK. He started breathing and crying after they prodded and warmed him a bit, and he is now a perfectly healthy ten-year-old. As an Investigator, he is part of the Fear Triad (also called the Thinking Triad). This strikes me as poetic, as I have never in my life experienced such primal fear as I did during those days surrounding his birth. I even remember thinking in those sleepless, terrifying seventy-odd hours that I was grateful for so rarely feeling such fear; it is a horrible emotion to endure. Fear, both this escalated life-or-death fear and more subtle daily scaredness, is the predominant driving emotion for the Thinking (or Head) Triad, enneagram types 5, 6, and 7.

## The Thinking Triad

Investigators, Loyalists, and Enthusiasts belong to the Thinking (or Head) Triad. These types take in their environment by assessing all the potential problems they may encounter. They use their minds to think through every possible scenario, believing they are creating order out of chaos. Whereas members of the Feeling Triad respond to the world by asking, "What do I feel?" members of the Thinking Triad respond by asking, "What do I think?"[1] Members of this triad are often exceptionally intelligent and spend a great deal of time inside their own heads, contemplating options and detailing pros and cons for every decision. Enneagram types 5, 6, and 7 analyze and observe the world, constantly scanning for problems in need of solving. Importantly, they do not act or respond to something until they think first. Because of this, members of the Thinking Triad sometimes miss out on life or relationships because they are held back by gathering and analyzing information.

Investigators assume there are always more answers and bits of information to gather and consider. They view knowledge as protection, and more than anything, they despise incompetence.[2] Fives can pull back or avoid relationships, fearing that they will not have the resources to give others; they can sometimes assume a scarcity mindset, which can result in hoarding—emotionally, mentally, or physically. Investigators often guard their time and emotions fiercely, aware that every interaction is a withdrawal from their energy bank. They are often incredibly smart and knowledgeable, inventive and curious, but they can also weaponize their intellect, hurting others with sarcasm and cynicism, or purposefully withholding information. Inventors are a perfect embodiment of this type (though of course not all inventors are Investigators): they take in and analyze information, find creative solutions to problems that arise, and continuously assess data as it becomes available.

Loyalists assimilate information through thinking, but for them, it doesn't always help to make sense of the world or their situation. They continuously scan the environment for threats, anticipating the worst possible outcomes; they question everything and are often plagued by doubt.[3] It logically follows that many Loyalists are more comfortable joining than leading, often questioning their own capacity to make decisions and assume control. This type composes the bulk of groups, and they are—as their name suggests—fiercely loyal to organizations in which they believe. All Sixes seek security; some find it by joining groups, and others find it by creating groups and structures that provide stability for themselves and others. When I think of Loyalists, I conjure the mental image of a protest or rally: such events are filled with Sixes who believe so wholeheartedly in a cause that they will congregate in droves to support it. Much social and political progress can be attributed to Loyalists who powerfully band together to enact change.

Enthusiasts are eternally optimistic, waking each day to limitless possibilities. They are energetic, charming, and charismatic, but this peppy exterior often masks any dark emotions or fear they may feel. This type struggles with satisfaction. In fact, they often reframe things in real time to give life a rosier hue or more upbeat vibe. Enthusiasts are spontaneous and fun-loving, and they strive for happiness in everything they do; they are easily bored and avoid criticism. Since life is messy and filled with challenges and stressors that Sevens simply do not want to confront, this type can become paralyzed by stress or incapacitated by fear; sometimes, Enthusiasts turn to unhealthy coping mechanisms to avoid negative emotions. Comedians are a good example of the Enthusiast mindset, always cheerful and creating happiness. They are often uncomfortable with sadness, fear, or other challenging emotions and are quick to turn tears into laughter.

Members of the Thinking Triad absorb external data and use it to order their lives. However, such relentless assessment can be terrifying. Stabile suggests that this triad is often called the "fear triad," and when they lack knowledge, they experience pain and insecurity.[4] Of course, *everyone* experiences fear, not just members of the Thinking Triad. However, for these types, all the world's dangers and possibilities feel very real. Scanning the world for potential problems, pitfalls, and threats can be stressful, exhausting, and depressing for members of this triad. And, for our purposes, it can increase stress and promote fear, which is the driver of performance anxiety in Investigators, Loyalists, and Enthusiasts.

Before we get too far into this chapter, I want to acknowledge that the suggestions in this book may be particularly hard for members of the Thinking Triad to swallow. Stabile notes that these types try very hard not to be influenced by others' thoughts and suggestions. However, this ultimately leaves them open instead to being influenced by their fear.[5] Try thinking of this journey as a data-gathering mission—one in which you try (possibly uncomfortable) things to amass more information about yourself, your fears, and your performance anxiety. After all, there is nothing an enneagram type 5, 6, or 7 loves more than cold, hard facts.

## Fear

Fear is triggered by the mechanisms discussed in Chapter 1: the brain detects a threat, resulting in a release of hormones that ultimately encourage the actions of fighting, fleeing, or freezing. Social researcher Brené Brown defines fear as "a negative, short-lasting, high-alert emotion in response to a perceived threat, and, like anxiety, it can be measured as a state or trait. Some people have a higher propensity to experience fear than others."[6] We can probably all define fear for ourselves and how it presents in our own bodies. For me, it feels like a focused attack directly on my heart, radiating outward in pinprick tingles throughout my chest, to the tips of my ears and the top of my head. When I experience fear, I involuntarily hold my breath, freezing in the face of the unnerving sensation.

In his popular podcast *Huberman Lab*, Stanford neuroscientist Andrew Huberman helpfully differentiates between fear, stress, and anxiety and examines how they are interrelated. He suggests that fear is built out of the elements of a stress response, and therefore encompasses anxiety. However, one can experience stress apart from fear.[7] This perhaps helps to differentiate between "performance anxiety" and "stage fright," though sometimes these terms are used interchangeably without regard for the semantic nuances of each. Typically, when researchers refer to stage fright, they mean a sudden onset of fear and panic onstage, which ultimately contributes to a deterioration of the performance.[8] Though it may seem like splitting hairs to delineate between the two terms, I believe that some performers feel an abundance of *anxiety* surrounding performances (particularly those in the Feeling Triad), while others experience an abundance of *fear* during performances (particularly those in the Thinking Triad).

Repeated fear, like continued experiences of stage fright, can cause trauma. Performers may have specific traumatic encounters—negative performing experiences that are cemented in their memories. Or, they may experience trauma resulting from the general fear of performing, not stemming from specific negative events. Huberman proposes an operational definition of trauma, describing it as fear ingrained within the nervous system, reappearing at inopportune times.[9] If you've gotten this far in this book, it is likely that performance fears are embedded in your nervous system and show up at inconvenient, unwanted times. While everyone responds to fear differently, members of the Thinking Triad often respond by shutting down. Since Investigators, Loyalists, and Enthusiasts view the world through thinking, when fear strikes unexpectedly and quickly, they may not have enough time to gather data and formulate an action plan. These types rely on pre-planning for all contingencies, but when something goes wrong for which they have not calculated, the resulting fear can cause paralysis.

## Combating Fear

The good news is that humans can combat and even *extinguish* fears and traumas. As you may imagine, this requires a good deal of work, and though we may wish that the process would end with the extermination of a fear, it does not. After extinguishing a certain fear or trauma, it must be replaced and actively linked with a positive experience.[10] This is often easier said than done: it requires taking a negative memory or idea and intentionally integrating it with new, positive memories or responses. For example, if a performer experiences a specific negative event (like the one I shared in the Prologue—a memory slip in a recital), they can extinguish that fear through narrative retelling and recollection; then, they can associate the fear with new, positive responses, such as successful performing experiences. Eventually, the trauma will become associated with the positive response rather than the negative.

This is a complex process and safest undertaken with a professional therapist. However, if resources for psychotherapy are lacking, journaling or talking with a close friend or partner may be helpful. The basic idea is that one's fear response will be very high in the initial recounting of a fearful or traumatic event. The first time recollecting an experience, going into extremely vivid detail, one may even experience *more* fear than during the actual traumatic event. Through subsequent retellings, the fear response will lessen and eventually abate altogether. For example, when seeing a horror film for the first time, the fear response will be very high; if watched a hundred times, the viewer will likely become a bit bored of it and feel very little fear on the hundredth viewing. While it is tempting to relegate fearful situations to the recesses of our minds, research proves that acknowledging and examining them is exceedingly healthier and more productive.

However, the work cannot end there. Huberman stresses that we cannot simply acclimate to a fearful event, but we must also attach new positive experiences to it. He gives an example of a child in a near-fatal bike collision. After the encounter, the rider may be so fearful of repeating the trauma that they simply give up bike riding altogether. However, if they engage in repeated narrative retelling of that event (preferably within clinical therapy sessions), the fear response will eventually abate and ultimately extinguish. The crucial next step is linking that event with new, positive responses. After the fear has burned out and the child is able to resume bike riding, they must actively associate positive experiences *while keeping the past trauma in mind*. If the child begins to associate pleasant experiences with biking, such as riding to a friend's house or using the bike to get to events they enjoy, they can actually rewire the memory with new positive associations.[11] However, this must be done while intentionally holding in mind the past trauma. The child must consciously think to themselves that they are riding their bike and enjoying it, *despite* the past trauma of the collision.

These principles can be applied to the fear that drives performance anxiety. Performers may have specific traumatic events that elicit fear responses, or they may fear performing generally. In therapy (or journaling or talking with confidants), they can retell the narrative of the fear experience, going into as much detail as possible and mentally re-experiencing the situation in real time. Repeated retelling of this narrative will diminish the fear response; once extinguished, they must associate new positive experiences with performing. Perhaps beginning with music lessons or performing for one friend, performers can link these new positive associations by intentionally thinking, "I'm performing well and enjoying it, despite my past fears and traumas."

For performers in the Thinking Triad, the fact that fear and trauma can be reconditioned into novel positive responses is especially important because a single threat or bad experience causing intense fear can train the nervous system to perpetuate the fear.[12] This means that a *single* subpar performance or terrifying bout of stage fright can forever link performing with the fear response, in the same way that a single close encounter with a bear or snake conditions animals (including humans) to fear them into perpetuity. If performers do not confront and properly deal with the fear surrounding performance, they will perpetually be stuck in its vicious cycle.

## Fear and Courage Logs

Fear often appears when performers perceive a lack of autonomy. In *Fight Your Fear and Win*, Don Greene reminds that every performance is a risk. But, in the face of such risk, acknowledging that we have made an autonomous choice to perform is critical.[13] We always have choices, and if you're reading this book, you've chosen to perform. For all performers, the potential reward of performing outweighs the risk. A musician may not have chosen to perform a year-end jury, but they did choose to walk into the room and go onstage. They could have chosen to skip the fear-inducing performance, adjudication, or examination and deal with the consequences, but they didn't. Every time performers go onstage to perform, it's because they have *chosen* to do so. Reclaiming autonomy in these anxiety-inducing situations is incredibly powerful.

Greene proposes cultivating courage as the antidote to fear.[14] Since the Thinking Triad is a data-gathering bunch, it may be helpful for these members to amass some data surrounding fear and courage and how it affects their lives. In *Fight Your Fear and Win*, Greene suggests keeping a Courage Log, noting the fear-inducing situation or event, the action taken in response, and the result.[15] Identifying situations to exercise courage is important, and it is necessary to experiment with various levels of risk. The systematic logging of fears and courageous actions can provide a data set that helps develop courage and confidence in one's ability to overcome fearful situations.

I would suggest going even further with the data collection by keeping a separate Fear Log. While Greene's Courage Log does include an item line for noting the fear itself, it may be useful to further tease out the root, nature, and intensity of a specific fear. Huberman suggests that it is necessary to identify interoceptive versus exteroceptive fear signals and whether they appear in an appropriate ratio for a given fear-triggering situation. By this, he means questioning whether internal fear signals (what manifests during performance as stage fright) and external signals (audience response, performance stakes, potential consequences) are appropriately aligned. For example, if you walk out into the road and are nearly hit by a bus, it is appropriate for fear to kick into the highest gear—after all, the adrenaline fuels your legs to scramble out of the way, potentially saving your life. It is even appropriate to feel shaky and disoriented for the rest of the day and perhaps have a nightmare that evening. However, if you continue to feel the intense fear and its physical symptoms months later, your interoceptive fear signals are disproportionate to the past threat, and you have likely developed post-traumatic stress disorder (PTSD) and should seek professional intervention.

As data is so near to the hearts of many Investigators, Loyalists, and Enthusiasts, I would encourage keeping a Fear Log that includes a quantifiable score for the strength of interoceptive and exteroceptive fear signals. The log below uses a 10-point scale, in which 1 indicates a very mild fear response and 10 indicates an incredibly strong fear response: (See Table 5.1)

A Fear Log may be helpful for data-gathering types, as it quantifies fear and compares the strength of internal versus external fear signals. In the first situation, the performer's internal fear signals were decently aligned with the external signals, and the overall experience was positive. In the second situation,

Table 5.1 *Fear Log Documenting Occurrences of Fear and Internal/External Fear Signals Impacting Overall Results*

| Fear Trigger | Internal Fear Signals | External Fear Signals | Action/Result | Duration of Fear Signals | Overall: Positive or Negative? |
|---|---|---|---|---|---|
| 1. Performing a solo in studio class | 4—Pretty nervous, intrusive thoughts. | 2—Everyone is friendly and understands these are works in progress, low risk. | Played well, despite being scared. | Started fifteen minutes before class, disappeared after I played. | Positive |
| 2. Performing a difficult solo in orchestra | 9—SO scared—this is a huge solo and I was afraid I'd do badly and never get another solo opportunity. | 8—High stakes. I knew if I messed up, the conductor would be upset and give the next solo to someone else. | I played OK, but not great. Way more mistakes than I anticipated. | Scared for two days before the concert, and I felt bad after I played. The low mood lasted a long time, and I'm nervous for the next performance. | Negative |
| 3. Sight reading a solo for a composer in class | 9—I was really scared because I doubt my sight reading ability. | 1—This really wasn't important—it was just a class period, and everyone was sight reading and making mistakes. | I played pretty well, but it didn't feel great. | I didn't know it was going to happen, and I got really afraid when he asked me to sight read on the spot. I stayed nervous through class thinking he might ask me to sight read more. | Positive. I played well and proved that I could sight read in that situation. |

the performer realizes the performance is relatively high-stakes (whether that is true or simply the performer's perception, it nonetheless feels more important relative to other performances). The performance did not go especially well, and the lingering fear signals and labeling the event as "negative" suggest that it likely escalated to trauma that needs reframing, linking the event with new, positive responses so that it does not continue to perpetuate future fear. In the third situation, the performer's interoceptive signals are clearly misaligned with the exteroceptive. Nevertheless, the event was a net positive, and the performer can use this data to inform more appropriate relationships between internal and external fear signals in the future.

Often within performance settings, performers fear failure or defeat. Greene reminds that we cannot succeed without taking risks, but the mere fact that we persevere in the face of fear demonstrates courage.[16] A Fear and/or Courage Log documents courageous actions taken in the face of fear. It proves that as performers, we are in fact risk-takers, and hopefully most performing situations are overall positive experiences. Furthermore, a written log can become a symbol of courage, reminding us of successful courageous acts in future fearful situations.[17] Symbols can become further data for the Thinking Triad; a program from a successful concert or an encouraging note from a teacher or colleague can serve as a physical reminder of courage and successful risk-taking. Performers in this triad may wish to gather these symbols into an album that they consult as part of their pre-performance ritual.

## Procrastination and Practice Mapping

Nearly everyone procrastinates to some extent, but for members of the Thinking Triad, procrastination can be particularly challenging. Since these types often spend so much time gathering and assessing data, Investigators, Loyalists, and Enthusiasts sometimes get stuck in the interminable thinking and deliberation process, which can impede action. A 1995 study showed that 70 percent of students procrastinate in completing academic tasks like writing papers, studying, and so on.[18] While this study did not specifically take into account performers' procrastination in terms of learning music, studying lines, or mastering dance moves, we can infer that performers also face a similar rate of procrastination within their own performance areas. While it is tempting to excuse procrastination as a normal part of life, it can nonetheless have serious repercussions on mental health. Avoidance not only increases stress but can also lead to depression and lowered self-esteem.[19]

For members of the Thinking Triad, fear can cause procrastination. If fear becomes overwhelming and one fixates on potential failure, they risk not acting at all.[20] Perhaps you've heard of the best-selling book *Eat That Frog!* by Brian Tracy. The author suggests several helpful tips (twenty-one, to be exact) to combat procrastination. While I will not review all of these, I find some of his advice particularly helpful for members of the Thinking Triad who struggle with decisive action when facing information overload. Tracy suggests that the first step is to arm yourself with three important qualities, the Three Ds: making a decision, disciplining oneself, and doing it with determination.[21] Several of the tips found in *Eat That Frog!* are similar to suggestions I give students regarding good practice habits. While it may seem like common sense, research proves that making physical lists and assigning imaginary deadlines increases productivity. Likewise, working on a daunting task in small chunks is preferable, and avoiding distraction is key.

For regular rehearsals, I encourage mapping out practice sessions. To do this, performers block out a long chunk of time (preferably 90–120 minutes) and divide it into fifteen-minute segments. Then, they assign specific tasks to each fifteen-minute block—the smaller, the better. For example, a student may spend the first block on a single phrase of music, focusing on phrasing, articulation, technique, accuracy, and so on. During these fifteen minutes, they are instructed to be hyper-focused—phone silenced and out of reach, concentrating intently on the defined task. When the timer rings, they can take a quick break, check their phone, get a drink, or stretch. The next fifteen-minute block must be entirely different; it cannot be an extension or repetition of the first. Perhaps they will concentrate on a new section of the same piece, or maybe they will switch songs/genres/techniques altogether. At the end of every four fifteen-minute blocks, I suggest an additional fifteen-minute block to review everything they've previously practiced. I also encourage adding one unassigned practice block after the review, to allow extra work on any problems that arose during the review. This sort of time chunking and intentional practice is extremely productive and encourages intense focus for brief periods of time, rather than aimlessly wandering through lengthy, unproductive practice sessions.

## The Work

Already Investigators, Loyalists, and Enthusiasts have several assignments. First, identify fears and traumas, extinguish them through narrative retelling, and assign them novel positive responses. Then, amass data through Courage and Fear Logs and assess the appropriateness of the ratio between interoceptive and exteroceptive fear signals and responses. Members of the Thinking Triad must also determine when fear is limiting, particularly when it causes paralysis or procrastination. Engaging in conscious risk-taking and combating procrastination will further aid in amassing data that proves courage; eventually, this data can serve as a physical symbol of courage.

While these tasks may seem extensive, the enneagram provides even more work for Investigators, Loyalists, and Enthusiasts to further understand themselves and what makes them tick. Here is some additional work for each specific type, which may be best explored in a journal dedicated to better understanding your performance anxiety:

### *Type 5: Investigators*

- Commit to spending time with others and fostering relationships that are important to you.
- Set concrete time limits for tasks you might lose yourself in, realizing your tendency to explore endless possibilities and ask "just one more" question.
- Schedule alarms and reminders to ensure that you are on time for important events.
- Make lists of pros and cons and set an endpoint for your research, trusting that you have investigated enough to make an informed decision.
- Trust your decisions, rather than ruminating on "what ifs."
- Know that others value your input and expertise, but they also value your feelings.

- Learn to identify your emotions and share them with those you trust.
- Notice when your mind races needlessly and find calming exercises for self-soothing, such as meditation or deep breathing.
- Develop a deeper understanding of and connection with your body; consider a physical routine like stretching, yoga, or tai chi.
- Recognize when your finite energy store is depleted, and preemptively ration to ensure sufficient energy for activities and people you value.

## Type 6: Loyalists

- Seek out groups and causes in which you believe, and devote your time and energy to them.
- Know that you are capable and intelligent, able to handle tricky situations on your own.
- Learn to engage in healthy disagreement and conflict with others. You can still respect and love those with whom you disagree.
- Realize that you cannot plan for all contingencies. Reality is messy, and things will go wrong despite your meticulous planning and organizing.
- Actively practice relaxing, perhaps through meditation or prayer.
- Notice all the things that end up working out, rather than resulting in worst-case scenarios.
- Identify when you are testing, judging, or distrusting others. Is it warranted?
- Evaluate whether remaining in certain relationships or situations is beneficial and healthy, or whether you persist simply out of duty or loyalty.
- Notice when you have overcommitted yourself; set boundaries for your time and energy.
- Remain present in the moment, rather than anticipating future problems.
- Cultivate a safe, stable inner calm that you can access in the midst of external chaos.

## Type 7: Enthusiasts

- Write to-do lists and set timers to accomplish necessary tasks.
- Practice spending and enjoying time alone.
- Decide which hobbies, activities, and groups are truly fulfilling, and dedicate your time and resources to them.
- Be aware that you fear missing out; prioritize those things that are truly important and worthwhile.
- Experiment with unstructured time, resisting the urge to fill every minute.
- Explore your emotions and truthfully examine the past, possibly through a journaling practice.
- Recognize that others may need a slower pace, time alone, or a lighter schedule.
- Identify difficult, darker, or complex emotions. Note when you feel sad, afraid, depressed, anxious, or hurt, and allow those emotions to unfold.
- Keep a gratitude log, appreciating the good in even the most mundane moments.
- Know that others will love and support you even if you are sad or unhappy.

I believe that everyone can profit from therapy, and members of the Thinking Triad may find particularly beneficial forms of therapy that specifically target fear or trauma, like CBT or EMDR; if fear appears suddenly in the form of panic attacks, ACT may be helpful (these types of therapy are defined in Chapter 2). Investigators, Loyalists, and Enthusiasts can also engage in visualization and mental reframing, which we will cover extensively in Chapter 8. Because these types are so attuned to their minds, mental practices like these may be particularly compelling. At the same time, physical movement can help members of the Thinking Triad feel more grounded within their bodies: simple practices like yoga, tai chi, or walking can integrate mind and body. While mostly an exercise of the mind, journaling is a tactile practice that facilitates the creation and retelling of narratives to extinguish fears. The good news for the Thinking Triad is that this work is effective; fear *can* actually be extinguished.

## Questions for Reflection

- How does fear manifest in your body? What physical feelings or sensations accompany this emotion?
- In your own experience, how is fear different from (or similar to) stress, anxiety, and other emotions?
- What have you read about your enneagram type that feels true to you? What does not?
- What proof do you have that you are a risk-taker? Do you have physical symbols of past courageous actions?
- Does procrastination impact your performance preparation? What tools can you use to lessen procrastination?
- Keep a Courage and/or Fear Log for one week. Mark every instance of fear and courage, and use the completed logs as data or symbols of courage.
- Assess how you deal with stressful or fearful situations. Do you notice a tendency to *think* about these situations rather than to *feel* during them?

## Notes

1. Stabile, *Journey*, 64.
2. Don Richard Riso and Russ Hudson, *Discovering Your Personality Type: The Essential Introduction to the Enneagram* (Boston: Houghton Mifflin, 2003), 128.
3. Riso and Hudson, *Discovering*, 137.
4. Stabile, *Journey*, 66.
5. Stabile, *Journey*, 67.
6. Brené Brown, *Atlas of the Heart* (New York: Random House, 2021), 12.
7. Andrew Huberman, "Erasing Fears and Traumas Based on the Modern Neuroscience of Fear," episode 49, Decemebr 6, 2021, *Huberman Lab*, Scicomm Media, https://www.hubermanlab.com/episode/erasing-fears-and-traumas-based-on-the-modern-neuroscience-of-fear (accessed March 3, 2024), 7:45.

8. Yaroslav Senyshyn, "Perspectives on Performance and Anxiety and Their Implications for Creative Teaching," *Canadian Journal of Education* 24, no. 1 (1999): 31.
9. *Huberman Lab*, "Erasing Fears," 8:35.
10. *Huberman Lab*, "Erasing Fears," 45:30.
11. *Huberman Lab*, "Erasing Fears," 59:10.
12. *Huberman Lab*, "Erasing Fears," 37:10.
13. Don Greene, *Fight Your Fear and Win* (New York: Broadway Books, 2001), 93.
14. Greene, *Fight Your Fear and Win*, 88.
15. Greene, *Fight Your Fear and Win*, 99.
16. Greene, *Fight Your Fear and Win*, 89.
17. Greene, *Fight Your Fear and Win*, 100.
18. H. C. Schouwenburg, "Academic Procrastination: Theoretical Notions, Measurements, and Research," in *Procrastination and Task Avoidance: Theory, Research, and Treatment*, ed. J. R. Ferrari, J. L. Johnson, and W. G. McCown (New York: Plenum, 1995), 71.
19. Dobson and Dobson, *Evidence-Based Practice of Cognitive-Behavioral Therapy*, 103.
20. Greene, *Fight Your Fear and Win*, 89.
21. Brian Tracy, *Eat that Frog!: 21 Great Ways to Stop Procrastination and Get More Done in Less Time* (Oakland: Berrett-Koehler, 2017), 5.

# 6 Anger
## *The Doing Triad (Reformers, Challengers, and Peacemakers)*

When my son was in second grade, he started struggling with black-and-white thinking in an interesting way. He has always been a rule follower, and he prefers when guidelines are clear and there is no gray area whatsoever. So when a soccer game didn't feel exactly like soccer practice, he had a hard time summoning flexible thinking to know "the right thing" to do. Similarly, when on a rare occasion he found himself not knowing what to do in a scholastic situation, my brilliant and deep-thinking son became immediately overwhelmed. I contacted the school counselor, and she met with me for a session before she started working with him. During the course of the wildly uncomfortable (for me) meeting, she asked, "What happens at home when you and your husband argue and yell? Or when you cry in front of the kids?" I stopped her right there. I think I actually held up my hand for her to halt. "I'm sorry," I said, shaking my head incredulously, "Are you suggesting that we are *supposed* to be going around yelling and crying at home?"

My husband and I lead a very level-headed, even-keeled life. As I told the school counselor, I doubt my children have ever heard yelling or arguing at home. She pursed her lips and handed me a laminated chart of anthropomorphized emotions—little red heads with stick-figure limbs depicting the "hot" emotions, blue heads for the "cool" ones, and so forth. She suggested we work on identifying emotions with sentences like, "When _____, I feel _____." At night, I would lie in bed with the kids talking about how we felt during the day *when*. . . . This lasted approximately five bedtimes, and our emotions mostly centered around shame, sadness, fear, and anxiety—exactly what you'd expect of a trio of types 3, 4, and 5.

For me, it is hardest to identify with the Anger Triad (also called the Doing Triad), which encompasses Challengers, Reformers, and Peacemakers. I try hard to avoid conflict, and any anger I feel usually morphs seamlessly into anxiety or shame. Truthfully, I envy those who can summon anger as fuel to enact meaningful change. When my heart breaks and I rage against the ceaseless injustices in our world, I tend toward depressive hopelessness and inaction. I admire those who generate anger and use it to make the world better, as many Ones, Eights, and Nines do.

## The Doing Triad

Reformers, Challengers, and Peacemakers make up the Doing (or Gut) Triad. Their names suggest action—reforming, challenging, peacemaking—and that is how this triad sees the world, though the question "What needs to be done?"[1] They progress through the world identifying things that need doing, either by themselves or others. While the Thinking Triad thinks before they act, the Doing Triad often does before they think, which can sometimes cause conflict or be counterproductive. However, wildly successful, charismatic leaders also hail from this triad, thanks to the quick action and instant decisiveness of many of its members. Reformers, Challengers, and Peacemakers are often excessively busy, with the energy to do whatever they set their minds to. Their intuition is reliable and typically ever-clear, earning this triad the alternate label of the Gut Triad.

In enneagram study, Ones are often named Perfectionists rather than Reformers. This type is committed to integrity and serving others, but they also suffer from a vindictive inner voice that criticizes them and others relentlessly. This type earns the title Reformer because its members strive to help, change, and restore the entire world to its full glory. Ones have exceptionally high expectations for themselves and others, are terrified of making mistakes, and will work relentlessly on whatever tasks they approach. Many musicians have seen the movie *Whiplash* (2014), which exemplifies the dark side of the Reformer personality. In it, an ambitious jazz drummer faces abuse and constant criticism from a perfection-driven instructor. Reformers are often incredibly successful and goal-oriented, but perfectionists suffer from vicious inner critics, never satisfied that they are good enough.

Challengers are forces of nature. They are exceptional friends and leaders, and they have the intelligence and fortitude to carry out staggering feats. Eights are capable of great collaboration, but they can become domineering and demeaning, pushing others out of their orbit. They are full of energy and always busy, and their combined dreams, stamina, and charisma can truly change the world. However, Challengers can be stubborn, impatient, and aggressive when stressed, hurting others and themselves. The 2006 film *The Devil Wears Prada* features a Challenger in action. Meryl Streep's brilliantly played character is the true definition of a Boss: Miranda is assertive, decisive, dominating, brilliant, and successful at all costs. Happily, over the course of the movie, this Challenger changes (to a degree) as she considers the emotions and circumstances of others.

Peacemakers are natural mediators, able to see all perspectives and truly appreciate and respect the various sides of any argument. They are naturally generous and unselfish, seeking agreement and common ground. However, Nines are easily distracted and can struggle to make decisions, and they often put others above themselves so drastically that they forget themselves entirely. When stressed, they can tend toward passive aggression, but when healthy, they are inclusive and inspiring. Some argue that Fred Rogers was a Helper (type 2), and that label is certainly fitting. But I agree with those who classify him—or at least his TV persona—as a Peacemaker. *Mr. Rogers' Neighborhood* taught millions of children to value their emotions and work harmoniously with others. When I think of peacemaking, I envision the powerful 1969 on-air moment when Mr. Rogers rolled up his pant cuffs and shared a wading pool with the Black Officer Clemmons.

Members of the Gut Triad are action-oriented; they focus on accomplishing tasks and keeping themselves and others safe. It frustrates Reformers, Challengers, and Peacemakers to stop and take time to think things through, as it steals time from actually *doing*. And, for this triad, feelings can seem unnecessary and unhelpful. Because these types demand control and want to be seen as strong, they value decisiveness and avoid vulnerability by avoiding emotions that make them feel weak.[2] Ones, Eights, and Nines need to intentionally allow thoughts and feelings to exist, realizing their lives will be fuller and richer if their minds and hearts undergird their actions.

When stressed, members of the Doing Triad seek to assign blame. They often blame themselves first and foremost, but they can quickly shift blame externally and lash out at others. Reformers, Challengers, and Peacemakers intuitively read rooms and people, absorbing their surroundings through the lens of intuition. They effectively scan their environments for what needs doing, but they respond to what they learn in different ways. Reformers look for problems, seeing immediately whatever is wrong or out of place. Challengers search for who is in charge and how they will respond to provocation, and Peacemakers seek a place to fit in and conflicts to avoid.

It might be surprising to learn that for all members of this triad—Peacemakers included—anger is the dominant emotional reflex. While anger is the emotion to which Reformers, Challengers, and Peacemakers naturally tend, they do not all experience it in the same way. Ones will let anger fester into resentment, Eights will express their anger and make it known, and Nines tend toward passive aggression.[3] Here we arrive at the linchpin for the Doing Triad: anger. Anger is a powerful driver of performance anxiety, and members of this triad must engage in serious work to manage it. The good news is that these three types have endless energy for the task.

## Anger

Anger is perhaps the most complex feeling examined in this book. Even emotion researchers disagree about the nature of anger and whether it is a primary or secondary emotion (an emotion fueled by or in response to another emotion). Nonetheless, we can probably all describe what anger feels like in our own bodies. I first notice anger behind my eyes, pulsing and thrumming until my entire head is buzzing; my jaw clenches and my focus narrows onto whatever has caused the unwanted emotion. In Chapter 1, we studied the physiology of the fight-or-flight response, spurred by adrenaline. When this "fight-or-flight" stress response was initially coined by Walter B. Cannon in 1915, scientists did not yet know that anger and fear could effectively be differentiated.[4] While the stress response mechanism for anger is the same as that which we studied in relation to fear, the resulting emotion and physical expression of anger are markedly different.

Interestingly, while animals display only two responses to threatening stimuli (rage and fear), humans "may experience three: anger directed outward (the counterpart of rage), anger directed toward [one]self (depression), and anxiety, or fear."[5] Research has further proved that fear and anger manifest differently within the human body. In a compelling study undertaken at New York Hospital, researchers found that the stomach lining of angry patients presented as red and inflamed, whereas the stomach lining of depressed or scared patients was pale.[6] Indeed, the Gut Triad's driving emotion riles the stomach; other studies examined later in this chapter suggest that anger impacts the body in several other perilous ways.

At its most fundamental level, anger is a response to a threat, which causes animals (humans included) to respond in a self-protective way. However, anger is arguably much more complex than an automatic stress response. Brené Brown suggests that anger appears when we believe that something unjust has occurred.[7] In this definition, unfairness and injustice lie at the heart of anger, warranting blame. When blame enters the equation, anger becomes particularly dangerous. We feel something must be done to hasten resolution, so we assign blame: to ourselves, to others, or to external circumstances.

Brown notes that when we feel anger, we innately want to respond with action.[8] This is particularly the case for the Doing Triad. Its members are typically ready to engage, rolling up their sleeves to get down and dirty with this hefty emotion. Perhaps you are familiar with the work of Gary Chapman, author of the popular *The Five Love Languages*. In a subsequent publication on anger, Chapman defines that anger is fueled by negative emotions and is the antithesis of love.[9] Perhaps you are beginning to see how easily anger can develop in performance. When disappointment or embarrassment appears in response to a misstep or mistake, anger quickly slides in, fueling the vicious cycle of performance anxiety.

## Anger and Health

Reformers, Challengers, and Peacemakers experience anger in very different ways. Because Ones survey the world for errors and problems that need fixing, they are often angered by these injustices; that anger morphs into resentment toward others who do not feel similarly incensed. Challengers routinely experience rage and are unafraid of direct conflict. Peacemakers suffer from unresolved anger, tending toward passive aggression rather than outright conflict. But, all three types must work to resolve and mitigate the anger bubbling under the surface because this emotion is unequivocally dangerous to physical, emotional, and mental well-being.

We will discuss anger and rage in relation to the mind-body connection in Chapter 8, but research proves that anger—particularly unexpressed anger—is incredibly harmful physically and mentally. A host of physical symptoms and diseases accompany anger, and suppressing anger eventually leads to physiological and psychological stress:

> A growing amount of evidence suggests that suppressed anger does relate to hypertension and heart disease. . . Findings also confirm a link between aggressive behaviors and painful muscle tension. In the case of heart disease, suppressed hostility is also an implicated factor. . . Suppressed anger can also give rise to increased worry and anxiety.[10]

For members of the Doing Triad who feel the work proposed in this book is trite or a waste of time, please consider that our health is at stake when anger is left to its own devices. We may believe we can handle anger; perhaps it does not currently impact your health in noticeable ways. However, a lifetime of angry moments—like a performer's career of anger flares accompanying performance anxiety—inevitably compounds and jeopardizes physical and mental health.

In her groundbreaking and enlightening book *Rage Becomes Her: The Power of Women's Anger*, Soraya Chemaly reveals that for many reasons, women internalize more anger than men. We will discuss gender in Chapter 9, including the fact that the male/female binary is incomplete and often unsuitable. Putting that conversation momentarily on hold, Chemaly notes that due to cultural norms, gendered expectations, and a host of other problematic reasons, women are more likely to experience significant health-related issues due to unexpressed anger:

> Women who repress their anger are twice as likely to die from heart-related disease. Responding with extreme rage, however, is similarly problematic. Two

hours after a vitriolic outburst, the risk of a heart attack increases fivefold, and the chance of suffering a stroke, fourfold. People with chronically elevated blood pressure of hypertension have a notable inability to express anger confidently and effectively.[11]

Additionally, anger impacts the immune system; one study finds that people are more prone to contract the common cold following an anger event. Likewise, women who repress their anger are three times more likely to suffer from autoimmune diseases and even cancer.[12] I urge all performers in the Gut Triad—and particularly those who are female—to read *Rage Becomes Her* in full; it is not mere hyperbole to say that your life may depend on it.

## Defusing Anger

It is important to remember that everyone experiences anger, not just members of the Doing Triad. However, as Reformers, Challengers, and Peacemakers tend most easily to anger, it is crucial that these types learn to deal with and defuse anger properly. In *Anger*, Gary Chapman outlines concrete steps for responding to anger in a healthy and productive way, including identifying ways in which we can take constructive action. The first step in dealing with anger is to notice the anger and consciously note its presence. Chapman notes that as silly as it sounds, mentally admitting you are angry is essential. Then, we must do whatever it takes to restrain our reflexive response—whether that is counting to 100 or forcing distraction, anger must not maintain the upper hand. Next, we must take time to enter the Thinking Triad's wheelhouse, assessing and listing all possible options. Finally, we enact the solution that will best serve all involved.[13]

While these five steps may seem like common sense, I would encourage giving them the old college try the next time you experience anger. Importantly, these steps transmute anger from *destructive* to *productive*, which can actually improve performance. Thus far in this chapter, anger has gotten a relatively bad rap. But, Chemaly and other emotion researchers suggest it is neutral, as is every emotion, and should not be avoided.[14] In fact, anger is powerful; it is energy that can be optimized and harnessed to enhance performance.[15] Similarly, Brown encourages that anger can be transformed for good.[16] But, how exactly do we do that?

Chapman's five steps are effective for transforming anger into something productive. However, the time and mental resources necessitated by this approach are perhaps best suited to non-performing situations. For anger that appears onstage fueling performance anxiety, a simpler, shorter approach is needed. In these critical moments, I suggest another of Chapman's techniques—this one is only two questions. When anger appears in performance, ask whether the anger response is both positive and loving.[17] In my experience with performers prone to onstage anger, it almost never appears in a positive or loving context. Often, they mentally explode: *My pianist is an effing idiot. Have you considered actually learning the right notes? God, what a total nightmare. This audience sucks.* This quick-fire fury can be directed at oneself, others, or external circumstances. While it is certainly a response to anger, it is definitely neither positive nor loving.

These questions require an objective assessment of anger. In asking whether a response is positive, we must determine whether the anger can trigger effective change. Asking whether a response is loving questions whether the anger is valid, designed to benefit oneself or others. Righteous anger appears when we notice victims of injustice or feel incensed when life is truly unfair; this type of anger is actually helpful. In these instances, members of the Doing Triad can quickly identify the action needed to resolve (or at least mitigate) the inequity. However, in performance, anger is not typically positive or loving; it usually appears as a maladaptive coping mechanism to prevent us from feeling other, more tender feelings.[18] When anger rears its ugly head during performance, performers should ask whether their response is positive and loving; if it is not, they must actively work to release it.

This is, of course, easier said than done. For members of the Doing Triad, anger is nearly impossible to dismiss. However, Reformers, Challengers, and Peacemakers are up for daunting tasks and armed to the hilt with stamina for the journey. I suggest that these types perform a mental checklist every time anger appears, both onstage and off. This checklist is quick and effective in a performing situation. First, acknowledge and identify anger when it presents itself. As Chapman suggests, name the emotion: *I am angry*. Then, ask whether the response is positive and whether it is loving. That's it. If anger during performance is neither positive nor loving, we must set it aside. This does not mean ignoring or repressing it forever, but it does mean that we are not allowed to deal with it in real time. After the performance, we can gather our list of grievances and go through the longer five-step process to assess and transform anger into something productive.

## Internal versus External Anger

In the study of New York Hospital patients mentioned earlier in this chapter, researchers determined that anger in humans is expressed in three ways: directed outward (rage), directed inward toward oneself (which researchers labeled as depression), or funneled into anxiety or fear. Importantly, these types of anger are generated via different hormones: research suggests that outward-focused anger is fueled by noradrenaline, whereas internal expressions of anger like depression and anxiety are fueled by adrenaline.[19] While all members of the Doing Triad tend toward anger as their driving emotion, it is possible that hormone expression differs between the three types, which may account for the different ways in which Reformers, Challengers, and Peacemakers experience and express it.

People deal with anger in myriad ways, depending on their personality and the circumstances in which anger appears. Some may tend toward denial or repression, while others may turn combative and mean. Others might engage in sarcasm or passive aggression, which we will examine later. All of these coping mechanisms can be focused either internally or externally, particularly within the context of performance. For members of the Doing Triad, performance anxiety often stems from anger directed at oneself. Chapman clarifies that we direct anger inward because we believe we are somehow the guilty party and the ones who have caused things to go wrong.[20] When Reformers, Challengers, and Peacemakers sense they have failed or underperformed, they often seethe with self-focused anger.

Performers suffering from self-directed anger must engage in a lifelong battle to combat it. This internal anger is pernicious and ruthless, and if left unchecked will often result in violence toward others or depression within oneself. In these instances, performers must utilize the checklist suggested earlier: identify anger and ask whether it is valid and productive. However, Chapman adds an additional, and arguably more difficult, step for internally focused anger: *forgiveness*.[21] Members of the Doing Triad may scoff at this suggestion, but it is imperative to forgive—rather than berate—oneself. This final step is particularly important within a performing context. Anger can endlessly generate more anger; it is a fire that deeply desires to keep burning and growing. But, berating and belittling oneself within performance always proves unproductive and detrimental. Members of the Anger Triad must remember that anger is only productive if we choose to learn from it, transforming it into a positive mechanism for change.

External anger may be explosive and evident, particularly when Challengers are involved. The other types, however, may tend toward more subtle (but equally devastating) expressions of external anger, like sarcasm and passive aggression, which are closely linked.[22] Given what we know about Reformers and Peacemakers, we can likely understand why these two types may be prone to less direct forms of anger expression. The word "passive" often conjures synonyms like "acquiescent" or "resigned," but when paired with aggression, these words do not get at the heart of the disastrous consequences of this behavior. Possibly, women tend toward passive aggression more than their male counterparts, in part because it is more culturally accepted for women to be indirectly aggressive.[23] For all who tend toward passive-aggressive behavior, the only solution is to learn instead how to deal with anger openly and directly.

Enneagram experts Riso and Hudson caution that anger is extremely powerful, but not inherently a bad or negative emotion. However, when unaddressed and unresolved, anger can cause lasting, monumental problems. They suggest that over time, unaddressed anger can lead to a constant, underlying feeling of agitation:

> It is important to remember that the response of anger itself is not the problem. Anger occurs spontaneously when we feel that someone or something is threatening our integrity.... But when we are not present to our anger, we resist its natural unfolding and become tense, frustrated, and resentful. Over time, this simmering frustration becomes an underlying feeling that is always with us.[24]

Many performers suffer from this constant, low-level anger, directed either internally or externally. In order to encourage the productive dissipation of anger, we must learn to recognize and deal with it effectively.

The steps Chapman outlines, listed earlier in this chapter, offer a process for dealing with anger directly. Additionally, he suggests steps for dealing with long-term anger, which has not unfolded appropriately; be aware that this list may be significantly harder to approach. The first step in this process is to make a physical list of everyone who has wronged us, recently or otherwise. Performers who regularly face internal anger must include themselves on this list. Then, we must analyze how we responded to each event or person. Has the anger been handled properly, the right action taken, and resolved in a positive, loving way? If not, Chapman suggests reconciliation—this might mean reconciling with the person or reconciling a past event or offense within our own minds, finally releasing it.[25] In Chapter 8, we will further explore the damaging effects of unresolved anger and rage; rest assured, it is in our best interest to tackle any residual anger we may be harboring.

## The Work

Reformers, Challengers, and Peacemakers have some heavy lifting to do in dealing with their primary emotion of anger. Already they have been tasked with several things: identifying and naming anger when it appears and asking whether the response is positive and loving. They must also notice when anger requires further action, going through the five steps Chapman suggests for transforming it into positive action. These types must be cautious of allowing anger to seep out in the form of sarcasm or passive aggression, which are harmful to self and others. Because anger is so dangerous—even deadly—to physical and mental well-being, members of the Anger Triad must be particularly vigilant in defusing this emotion properly.

For enneagram types 1, 8, and 9, anger can be an incredibly powerful tool for enacting change and motivating performance; as Brown suggests, anger can be creatively transformed into something positive. The goal for performers in this triad is not to allow anger to distract and disarm, fueling performance anxiety and internal judgment. Instead, Ones, Eights, and Nines must realize that they can harness anger for motivation, using it to fuel meaningful change. Anger makes people uncomfortable—it makes *us* uncomfortable. We often stuff it down through maladaptive coping mechanisms, resulting in feelings of hopelessness and futility, shame, and anxiety. Fortunately, this powerful emotion can be transformed and metabolized into beautiful, unfettered greatness.

While these assignments may seem enough to keep Reformers, Challengers, and Peacemakers busy for life, there is yet more to do, suggested by the enneagram for these types. Here is some additional work for each specific type, which may be best explored in a journal dedicated to better understanding your performance anxiety:

## *Type 1: Reformers*

- Challenge your inner critic; know that it is unreliable and dishonest.
- Realize that others may not know your systems, organizational processes, standards, or habits; they may not intend disrespect when they unknowingly break rules.
- Notice when you judge others and mindfully consider their ideas, opinions, and beliefs.
- Practice self-forgiveness.
- Allow time for play, rest, and fun, realizing that not all endeavors need to be serious, productive, or educational.
- Identify defensive tendencies and try to accept criticism with open-hearted curiosity.
- Maintain realistic standards and goals. Would you expect of others what you demand of yourself?
- Set time and energy boundaries for less important tasks, recognizing when "good enough" is sufficient.

## *Type 8: Challengers*

- Schedule time for rest and renewal, acknowledging your natural inclination to work and achieve unceasingly.
- Depend on others, trusting their work and value.
- Practice openness and examine feelings of vulnerability; consider working through vulnerable emotions with a therapist or in a journal.

- Transform anger into something productive, using it as fuel to effect meaningful change.
- Assess your stress level and mindfully consider how much you are realistically able to handle.
- Resist the urge to change others.
- Notice when you view others as competitors or situations as battles to be won.
- Know that others will respect and love you even in your vulnerable or unsuccessful moments.

## Type 9: Peacemakers

- Find meaningful, creative ways to express yourself; consider poetry, art, or dance.
- Notice when you suppress your true thoughts or opinions for fear of creating conflict.
- Identify and express anger and resentment, realizing you risk harming yourself by repressing unpleasant emotions.
- Set deadlines for yourself and break tasks down into small, manageable steps.
- Deal with problems directly, rather than ignoring them or hoping they will disappear.
- Determine what you believe, what is important to you, and what you want. Express your beliefs and opinions with confidence, even when others disagree.
- Do not agree to things or go along with plans contradicting your beliefs or desires.
- Know that relationships can survive disagreement and conflict.

Members of the Doing Triad can particularly benefit from calming techniques, such as mindfulness practices and exercises like the physiological sigh, covered in Chapter 10. Because these types are prone to action, physical exercise like walking and yoga can integrate body and mind. Additional exercise of higher intensity, if appropriate, may also help high-energy types feel more grounded and secure, both physically and emotionally. Because Reformers, Challengers, and Peacemakers have some difficulty accessing their thinking and feeling centers, therapy may be advantageous; thoughts and emotions can be addressed, acknowledged, and acted upon safely within a clinical setting. If these types are open to adopting a spiritual or meditative practice, these activities may further increase awareness of thoughts and emotions as they arise.

## *Questions for Reflection*

- How do you experience anger? What physical feelings accompany it?
- How does anger impact your performance?
- What have you read about your enneagram type that feels true to you? What does not?
- Consider implementing the in-performance checklist: identify anger and ask whether it is positive and/or loving.
- Can you see the value in Chapman's five steps to combat anger? How could you use this process when anger appears?
- What are some examples of unresolved anger in your life? What could you do to resolve these?
- What does it look like to forgive yourself, particularly within a performing context?

# Notes

1. Stabile, *Journey*, 20.
2. Riso and Hudson, *Discovering*, 157.
3. Stabile, *Journey*, 97–8.
4. Daniel H. Funkenstein, "The Physiology of Fear and Anger," *Scientific American* 192, no. 5 (May 1955): 74.
5. Funkenstein, "The Physiology of Fear and Anger," 74.
6. Funkenstein, "The Physiology of Fear and Anger," 74.

7   Brown, *Atlas*, 220.
8   Brown, *Atlas*, 220.
9   Gary Chapman, *Anger: Taming a Powerful Emotion* (Chicago: Moody Publishers, 2015), 18.
10  Mark P. Cosgrove, *Counseling for Anger* (Dallas: Word, 1988), 68.
11  Soraya Chemaly, *Rage Becomes Her: The Power of Women's Anger* (New York: Atria, 2018), 53.
12  Chemaly, *Rage Becomes Her*, 53–4.
13  Chapman, *Anger*, 53.
14  Chemaly, *Rage Becomes Her*, 260.
15  Lex Fridman, "Andrew Huberman: Relationships, Drama, Betrayal, Sex, and Love," episode 393, August 17, 2023, *Lex Fridman Podcast*, https://lexfridman.com/andrew-huberman-4/ (accessed March 14, 2024), 58:26.
16  Brown, *Atlas*, 224.
17  Chapman, *Anger*, 36–7.
18  Stabile, *Journey*, 108.
19  Funkenstein, "The Physiology of Fear and Anger," 77.
20  Chapman, *Anger*, 176.
21  Chapman, *Anger*, 176.
22  Willard Gaylin, *The Rage Within: Anger in Modern Life* (New York: Simon and Schuster, 1984), 104.
23  Chemaly, *Rage Becomes Her*, 19.
24  Don Richard Riso and Russ Hudson, *Understanding the Enneagram: The Practical Guide to Personality Types* (New York: Houghton Mifflin, 2000), 63.
25  Chapman, *Anger*, 111.

# 7 Nine Lives
## Performance Anxiety and the Enneagram

As humans, we take in the world through our senses. It is profoundly beautiful that we all do this in different ways: Feelers take in the world through the heart, Thinkers through the mind, and Doers through intuition (or the gut). These are our hardwired Centers of Intelligence, assigned by our very DNA. But, as mind-body guru Nicole Sachs notes, it is important to remember that our first response is merely a reflex; it is our second response over which we can execute control.[1] Members of the Feeling Triad will reflexively respond to triggers with shame, those in the Thinking Triad with fear, and those in the Doing Triad with anger. Those are our primal *reflexes*. The work of this book, however, is to engender healthier *second* reactions, which involves engaging the other two Centers of Intelligence. This chapter examines how each of the enneagram types may respond specifically to performance and how they can temper performance anxiety. In the face of this particular stress, we must actively regain balance and engage our non-dominant Centers of Intelligence.

## Type 1: The Reformer

Ones often suffer from perfectionist tendencies and harsh inner critics. In performance, Reformers hear this voice constantly reminding them they are never good enough; it points out every miniscule performance flaw. Ones are very concerned with others' perception, and as members of the Anger Triad, they may respond to devastating inner criticism with searing anger toward themselves. It is especially important for Ones to recognize the incongruence between internal and external cues. Often their internal criticism or self-imposed pressure does not align properly with the real, external performance circumstances.

Perfection is unattainable, and performance is *work*, not *self*. Reformers must tap into their thinking and feeling centers, rather than relying simply on what their intuition implies about themselves. Gathering data about past successes, collecting (and believing) compliments from trustworthy sources, and noticing and tending to feelings that arise is critical for this type in performance situations.

## Type 2: The Helper

Helpers are hyper-focused on dependability; these performers may feel as though they will let everyone down if they underperform. As a member of the Feeling Triad, Helpers are particularly prone to anxiety, and believing they are not only responsible to themselves (but also to every other person they've ever met) fuels anxiety exponentially. Because setting boundaries is difficult for Twos, they may expend so much time and energy giving to others that they do not have enough time for their own performance preparation and mental/physical/emotional tending; but shirking these tasks will undoubtedly compound performance anxiety.

Twos need to set boundaries protecting their time and energy, perhaps through a written practice schedule and performance timeline. Because they value relationships so heavily, this type may be especially compelled to dedicate specific performances or musical pieces to loved ones (a practice discussed later in this chapter). However, Helpers must determine their own motivation for performing, separate from what they believe others expect. It is essential that Twos determine what *they* truly want and make a concrete plan to achieve it.

## Type 3: The Achiever

This type is prone to perfectionism, Imposter Syndrome, high anxiety, and feelings of shame—all of which compound performance anxiety, adding fuel to an already roaring fire. Achievers must address shame and manage anxiety through meditation, journaling, therapy, and/or with the assistance of prescription medication. Additionally, Achievers must continually remind themselves that their performances are separate from their inner selves: criticism of one's work does not equate to failure of one's character. As Threes' orientation to time is the future, it is also important for this type to remain grounded in the present moment, rather than fretting over what may happen or anticipating what will be.

While Achievers attain greatness through dogged hard work and determination, they must also access their emotions and slow down enough to deal with them appropriately. Because they are so accustomed to providing what others need and want, Achievers may struggle to determine what *they* actually need and want. Identifying personal motivation for performing is essential for this type.

## *Type 4: The Individualist*

Individualists are endlessly creative and artistic, with lives full of exceptionally high highs and impossibly low lows. This type must seek balance and accept the predominantly "average" emotions and experiences; it is often in this mundane middle that humans find security and safety. Sometimes, performance anxiety can be fueled by this excessive concentration on extremes. Fours' orientation to time is the past, so this type must be cautious of their tendency to ruminate on past negative events or emotions or unhelpfully dredge up old traumas. As part of the Feeling Triad, Fours tend toward shame, particularly over past events. They must work to leave the past in the past and realize that previous negative performance experiences do not predict future outcomes.

Because Individualists strive to distinguish themselves as unique individuals, performers of this type may put undue pressure on themselves to stand out. Or they may believe their performance anxiety and emotions are unique; realizing that everyone struggles (to varying degrees) is part of the Individualists' work. Harnessing performance as a vehicle to express their true self is an exceptionally potent antidote to performance anxiety for Individualists.

## *Type 5: The Investigator*

Fives are observant and inquisitive, independent and profoundly perceptive. Part of the Fear Triad, Investigators may become paralyzed when their thoughtfully prepared performance plan is upended. Likewise, they may spend so much time gathering data that they procrastinate and have trouble taking decisive action. Performance anxiety for Investigators is fueled by fear, often resulting from the knowledge that they cannot control or predict all the variables within a performance setting. Investigators must gather more helpful data: evidence of past performance successes and lists of courageous things they have done. Because this type is part of the Thinking Triad, mental rehearsal, visualization, and reframing (practices covered in the next chapter) may be very beneficial in thwarting performance anxiety for Investigators.

Performers of this type must cultivate flexible thinking, which allows them to respond to unexpected occurrences during performance in real time. Furthermore, Investigators must be aware that they have limited energy for each day; performance requires exceptional stores of mental, emotional, and physical energy, so they must protect their time and energy in order to perform their best. At the same time, because social interaction is not always a priority for Fives, they must intentionally seek balance between their desire for solitude and their innate need for interpersonal connection.

## *Type 6: The Loyalist*

Sixes need to feel safe; performing is a risky endeavor, so it can spark fear, which drives performance anxiety. Because this type is prone to conjuring worst-case scenarios and their own hypothetical responses, Loyalists must allow themselves to think briefly about *What if?* and then examine and trust the empirical data from previous performances—typically, the worst-case scenario will not play out and doomsday prepping proves unnecessary. In performance, Sixes need to trust their own ability and preparation, believing they have reliably prepared and are fully capable of executing a successful performance on their own. Because Loyalists constantly scan the room for danger, they must be particularly aware of the balance between internal and external fear signals during performance and notice when their perception of external signals is skewed.

In *The Road Back to You* by Ian Morgan Cron and Suzanne Stabile, the co-authors suggest that Sixes frequently have complicated relationships with success.[2] Sixes often fear the spotlight; Loyalists also fear hurting others by competing with them. This can all further fuel performance anxiety, so Sixes need particularly strong personal motivation for performing.

## Type 7: The Enthusiast

As part of the Thinking Triad, Enthusiasts believe they can intellectualize negative emotions. When performance fears arise, Sevens tend to avoid or back out of anxiety-producing situations altogether, or deny or numb the fears. Unfortunately, this type is particularly prone to addictions,[3] and they must take care to manage their emotions—both the positive and the negative—properly. When Sevens perform, they do so to entertain others and themselves. Their orientation to time is the future, and they may have difficulty remaining fully present in the moment, especially if the moment is tedious and mundane. This type benefits from a clear performance preparation checklist, particularly breaking down the "boring" parts of the practice routine.

As performers, Sevens are often more enchanted with the excitement and anticipation that precede performance, sometimes disappointed or let down by the actual performance, or depressed in the aftermath of such a momentous event. They are easily addicted to the brilliant spotlights and roar of happy audiences, so these performers must be particularly aware of just how far they can fall when a performance takes an unexpected turn. Exploring the full spectrum of emotions offstage and on is crucial for Enthusiasts.

## Type 8: The Challenger

Challengers have more energy than any other enneagram type. When performing, this type may use their energy to obsess and dominate, acting aggressive or controlling. Eights need to consciously expend energy during performance preparation, perhaps engaging in more physical exercise and mentally stimulating activities like reading or journaling. As a member of the Anger Triad, rage simmers below the surface for Eights; when performance anxiety or errors strike, Challengers often berate themselves or others, mentally or verbally. This type must assemble a toolkit for dealing with anger flares, particularly during performance; they may find grounding exercises helpful, mentally noting things they can see, hear, taste, smell, and touch.

Challengers are formidable in most aspects of their lives, including performance. It is often easy for Eights to power through performance preparation and simply do what must be done so the show goes on. However, performers of this type are prone to burnout and must also tend to their emotional and mental needs, hard as it may be to acknowledge and define them. Challengers are capable of greatness, but they must make and enforce reasonable deadlines and to-do lists for themselves. Sleep, mindfulness practices like meditation, and other calming and regenerative exercises are critical for Eights.

## Type 9: The Peacemaker

Nines tend to be extremely laidback, and this is often a positive trait. However, when performance demands effective preparation, this type can struggle with self-starting and may procrastinate. In performance preparation, this type must make goal lists and dedicate specific time and energy toward carrying out necessary tasks. Because their orientation to time is the past, Nines can dwell on mistakes during performance and allow them to negatively impact the performance moving forward.

Because Nines fear conflict and stress, they often withdraw from anxiety-inducing situations, at least emotionally. This type must consciously identify and express emotions, verbally stating what they need and want. Peacemakers avoid conflict and confrontation at all costs, so if Nines disagree with other members of a performing ensemble, they need to intentionally plan what they will say and how they will initiate the necessary conversation.

---

If you skipped through the other eight types to read only the section pertinent to you, I would encourage you to go back and examine the others as well. All nine enneagram types appear on every single stage, in every ensemble, as part of every dance company, on every basketball court, in every boardroom, and in every other performance situation you can imagine. These are our colleagues, teachers, audience members, castmates, friends, family, enemies—every person we will ever encounter. Understanding the enneagram more fully encourages compassion for ourselves and others, and it informs how we can best support and relate to other types.

Clearly, each enneagram type manifests and responds to performance anxiety differently. To tackle the shame, fear, and anger that drives anxiety, some types may respond best to mental exercises; others will benefit from physical engagement, and others from a closer examination of their feelings.

If you took the time to read how performance anxiety affects each of the nine types, you likely noted a repeated theme: all types must define for themselves very clear motivation to perform.

## Motivation

I would not recommend procreation just to lessen performance anxiety. But, having children was for me the biggest *performance* anxiety-reducing factor in my life thus far. I stress the word *performance* because parenting has unequivocally ramped up anxiety in other areas—I constantly think of ways in which my children could perish or worry I am ruining them with subpar mothering. If you read the chapter on fear, the story of my son's delivery may have been enough for you to swear off reproduction altogether. I wish I could tell you that my daughter's birth three years later was easy breezy, but alas, it was a similarly dramatic ordeal in which I nearly died. In any case, having children rocked my world in the way it rocks every new parent's world—suddenly, it wasn't all about me. In fact, my life hardly ever centered around me anymore. No matter how important a concert was, I went home and changed diapers and put babies to bed. They had no idea if I failed or succeeded, and frankly, they couldn't care less. My children remain wholly unimpressed by my profession. It is humbling, but also incredibly freeing.

Having faced the fear of losing them (and myself), I realized how inconsequential my performance mistakes really are. Don't get me wrong—I still care deeply about my art and put undue pressure on myself to perform well. But, at the end of the day, my children have impacted my *motivation* for performing. Motivation is a tricky thing, and one I discuss with students all the time. The *why* for performing is just as important—if not more so— as the *how*. Sometimes my students give flippant surface-level answers: "I'm performing a jury because you force me to at the end of every semester." I give them my perfected that-was-so-funny-now-cut-the-shit smile, and we get to the real work of trying to ascertain meaningful motivation. Motivation is such an incredibly important part of our work as performers because the *lack* of meaningful motivation can cause performance anxiety to skyrocket.

If I'm being honest, my motivation to perform during my student years was often incredibly shallow. I wanted to prove that I was exceptional. I craved admiration and applause. I now realize that as an Achiever, I am prone to seek worthiness and validation external to myself. This sort of hollow motivation increased my performance anxiety exponentially; it added pressure to perform perfectly to attain those fleeting end goals. So, how do we find more meaningful motivation that can help alleviate some anxiety to boot?

For me, the most meaningful motivators are people I love dearly and causes I believe in. My grandfather was a musician, and he loved to listen to me play. It didn't matter what I played, whether he liked the genre or had ever heard of the composer; he loved everything I presented, unwaveringly. I never felt nervous to perform for him because I knew that I couldn't disappoint him. His heartfelt applause was ever-present. Once, at the ripe performing age of nine, I played for him the accompaniment to Richard Marx's 1989 pop hit "Right Here Waiting." I did not sing the melody or attempt to present it in any way, so it was just a meandering series of arpeggiated chords. At the end, he jumped to his feet and yelled, "BRAVO!" so loudly that I was convinced to enter that piece (still *just* the accompaniment) in a Fourth of July talent show in which I did not place.

I often encourage students to assign musical pieces specific dedications. I ask them not to plan these ahead of time but to save the dedications for the moments right before a performance—often the exact time performance anxiety attacks. During the performance, the student then mentally dedicates each piece to someone important. When nerves hit, they focus on that loved one and imagine they are playing the piece only for that person, who will love them regardless of the outcome. I dedicate a lot of music to my late grandfather, and it eases my anxiety exponentially to imagine that he is somewhere in the Universe, beaming triumphantly at whatever music I offer.

Sometimes meaningful motivation arises from collaboration. Right after my son was born, one of my undergraduate professors, a saxophonist, invited me to collaborate on a conference recital. I was admittedly not in my best performing shape: I was grappling with new motherhood, scarcely finding time to bathe, let alone practice. Plus, this was a high-stakes recital, performing for other university music professors. I nearly declined, but I knew I would likely never have the opportunity to perform with her again. She meant a lot to me, and I truly wanted to accept her invitation. While I did find time to bathe before the concert, I did not unearth exactly as much rehearsal time as I would have liked. But, in the end I knew I was ready enough to perform. I focused on the opportunity I'd been presented with—I was grateful for this experience and wanted to glean whatever I could learn from it. I have heard similar stories from other performers—instrumentalists who reveled in the chance to play under a certain conductor, or singers who were grateful to perform a specific role. These opportunities may not arise again, and gratitude and open-hearted acceptance of the *gift* to perform can help alleviate anxiety.

Likewise, certain venues can be freeing for performers. I serve as the graduate advisor for the music school at my university, so I get to know the graduate population quite well. A few years ago, several of the graduate vocalists showed me a recording of a karaoke event they had attended. I was dumbfounded by their talent. I had seen them execute exquisite operatic performances, so I knew they were remarkable singers. But their eyes lit up with joy as they laughed, danced, and sang, free from the pressures of the university setting. I asked one of the students how it felt to perform so brilliantly, and she guffawed, "That? That's not *real* performing! That's just fun."

I feel the same when I play for funerals. Perhaps I should rephrase that, or at least give some additional context: I am a church musician, so I often provide music for weddings and funerals. I certainly do not have fun at funerals, but I find them utterly, heartbreakingly meaningful (I cannot always say the same for weddings). I have never felt nervous to play for a funeral, in large part because I do not consider it a performance—to me it is a calling, a vocation, an offering. If we can find the proper motivation or assign broader meaning to our performance—even if it is a semester-end jury—our performance anxiety will lessen significantly.

## *A Final Note on Motivation*

I would like to share an unpopular opinion here: it is OK if you perform because it is something you just happen to be good at. This book opens with my confession that I don't love performing, but I haven't yet admitted what I do love: a challenge. Learning and performing music is exceptionally challenging, and that is what I love. I landed in music because I am a very hard worker, and dogged hard work combined with my perhaps-higher-than-average musical talent made me a formidable performer. I can think of nothing so rewarding as successfully executing the physical, mental, and emotional feats of a musical challenge. It has taken me decades to realize that loving a challenge is a valid reason for performing.

It is equally OK to perform because you love it. I have many colleagues, friends, and students who absolutely adore performing and cannot imagine pursuing any other profession or endeavor. Likewise, I know performers who pursue other careers about which they are equally passionate, performing in less traditional ways or settings. Whatever *your* reason, you have a right to perform, and it is OK if your motivation differs from that of every other person you know.

## Spiritual Practices

My father recently retired from a long career of teaching high school. Throughout his thirty-three years as an educator, he taught courses in both science and religion. So, I grew up understanding that the two can co-exist and even complement each other. However, I was admittedly rather surprised when my favorite podcasting neuroscientist revealed his own spiritual practice of morning prayer. In an interview with Russian-American computer scientist Lex Fridman, Andrew Huberman suggested that believing in a higher power can restore a sense of agency.[4] You may not participate in organized religion, or you may firmly subscribe to agnosticism or atheism; I'm certainly not suggesting that you change who you are or what you believe. However, particularly as performers, we must realize we are never entirely in control. For many, some kind of spiritual practice can help in surrendering the illusion of control.

Enneagram guru Suzanne Stabile shares that she's always attended church and maintains an active spiritual life; she is married to a United Methodist minister. In fact, he is the creator of the prayer beads I mentioned earlier.[5] In her extensive writing on the enneagram, Stabile offers spiritual practices for each type. These are a way to be in relationship with the "higher power" Huberman mentions, but they are also a means to further understand oneself. Regardless of what sort of spirituality we claim (if any), actively relinquishing control is transformative. I encourage you to determine what sort of spiritual practices you might incorporate into your life, and whether there is room for the Divine on your journey.

## Social Connection

Nearly every researcher I have cited stresses the importance of social connection to mitigate anxiety, fear, shame, anger, and other unwanted emotions. Huberman states that isolation can cause or exacerbate fear and trauma, noting that social connection is scientifically proven to diminish unwanted feelings, resulting in real neuro-chemical effects within the brain.[6] Likewise, Stabile wrote an entire book on social connections: *The Path Between Us: An Enneagram Journey to Healthy Relationships* stresses the necessity of healthy interpersonal relationships. Brené Brown suggests that belonging is necessary and fundamental to human development.[7] Building social connections and fostering healthy relationships is integral to mitigating anxiety, and in order to establish and maintain those interpersonal connections, we must first fully understand and know ourselves, which is finally the purpose of this book. Self-understanding and social connection are innately linked; both are essential for all performers.

As performers, I suggest we view performance as a two-way relationship in which we receive as much as we give. This symbiotic view of performance strengthens social bonds and fosters connection, rather than assuming that the audience is antagonistic or judgmental. Brown suggests that healthy connections between people allow for criticism and growth, which can ultimately strengthen those relationships: "Connection is the energy between people when they feel seen, heard, and valued; when they can give and receive without judgment; and when they derive sustenance and strength from the relationship."[8] The ideal performing situation is just that—a safe space in which we feel fully seen and appreciated, respected for who we truly are, without judgment. That type of performing strengthens relationships and provides sustenance for a lifetime onstage.

## Questions for Reflection

- How does your enneagram type inform your experience of performance anxiety?
- What have you read that feels true about your enneagram type? What does not?
- Given what you know now about your personality, how can you better approach and manage performance anxiety?
- Create a list of things you want to try as you continue your performing journey.
- What is your motivation for performing? Does this change based on venue, event type, or other circumstances?
- What spiritual practices might you consider engaging in regularly?
- How can you foster meaningful social connections?

## Notes

1. Nicole Sachs, *The Cure for Chronic Pain*, https://www.thecureforchronicpain.com/anxietycourseintro (accessed March 13, 2024).
2. Ian Morgan Cron and Suzanne Stabile, *The Road Back to You: An Enneagram Journey to Self-Discovery* (Downers Grove: InterVarsity Press, 2016), 200.
3. Cron and Stabile, *The Road Back to You*, 212.
4. *Lex Fridman Podcast*, "Andrew Huberman," 60:00.
5. https://www.lifeinthetrinityministry.com/store.
6. *Huberman Lab*, "Erasing Fears," 61:15.
7. Brown, *Atlas*, 154.
8. Brown, *Atlas*, 170.

# 8 Letting Go
## *The Mind-Body Connection*

As a (recovering) perfectionist, I have sought to control every aspect of my life for as long as I can remember. In school, I studied harder than I needed to, pulling all-nighters already in middle school in order to feel completely "in control" when I took a test or wrote a report—nothing could surprise my over-prepared self. When I hit graduate school, I practiced into the wee hours of the morning, risking life and limb while walking through dangerous areas in the dark, and overtaxing my body and mind in an effort to control my performance outcomes. In my darkest hours, I have misused my skills at reading emotions to willfully manipulate others and control relationships to maintain the (perceived) upper hand. Throughout all of this, I engaged in a dangerous Russian roulette with an eating disorder which was, finally, an attempt to regain control while I was flailing wildly out of it.

Surprisingly to no one but me, none of this worked. When I was nearing forty and found myself facing a mild midlife crisis, I somewhat angrily reflected that I had done everything right! I had worked so hard and tried so many things and read every self-help book I could find, and still I was struggling. *Aren't you supposed to have life figured out by the time you hit forty?* I had the spouse and the house and the career and the kids, but I still couldn't control my anxiety or the eating disorder. I found myself lying in bed one night, unable to sleep as I ruminated on it all. I finally surrendered to trying the ONE thing I had always refused before: therapy.

We've already explored several aspects of well-being, including options for therapy, but the point here is that we need to arrive at the realization that we're not actually in control. Chapter 1 covered the voluntary and involuntary functions of the brain. It is prudent to remember which things we can control: our physical actions, our preparation, and our environment to a certain extent. We cannot control the involuntary sympathetic nervous system response we recognize as performance anxiety. The good news is that we can understand it better, and we can control our response once it is activated.

## A Tipping Point

Part of my eternal learning quest involves listening to an embarrassing number of podcasts, which you may already have noted. (A previous therapist suggested it was more a symptom of not being able to be alone in my head without voices constantly piping into my ears. We agreed to disagree.) One of the podcasts I listen to regularly is *The Cure for Chronic Pain* with Nicole Sachs. Now, I don't actually have chronic pain, so this may be somewhat confusing. But I did suffer from debilitating, unexplained pain in my shoulders during my first pregnancy. I saw multiple specialists, but they weren't able to do scans or X-rays on a pregnant patient, so their best guess was that somehow a hormonal shift loosened my ligaments and resulted in actual injury to both shoulders. Then, the pain spread to my elbows, and finally my knees. I could sleep only a couple hours at a time before the unrelenting pain woke me, and then I would take a scalding bath followed by icing my joints. Rinse (literally) and repeat. I spent months in this condition, and making music became excruciatingly painful and nearly impossible.

Unsurprisingly, the baby was eventually born, and I had cortisone shots in both shoulders and forgot about the joint pain while busy with my full-time job and identity crisis of becoming a new mom to a colicky, premature baby. And then, the intolerable shoulder pain would intermittently flare up. I visited numerous specialists and was subjected to dozens of blood tests; I saw rheumatologists and neurologists and was repeatedly given clean bills of health. I logged the pain religiously in a book. I tried relating it to my menstrual cycle. I noted the foods I ate when my shoulders ached. I chronicled every physical activity I engaged in. Nothing. No patterns. No explanation.

Until . . . Many years later, I was listening to another podcast (*My Favorite Murder*—any fellow Murderinos out there? SSDGM) and one of the hosts mentioned *The Cure for Chronic Pain*. I gave it a curious listen, and after a few episodes, I considered the unresolved shoulder pain that still occasionally plagued me. My mind was blown when I realized the pain was psychogenic.

It came into my life at an exceptionally stressful time, and it continued to flare when I was at breaking points of various kinds—*that* was the connection I hadn't seen, the pattern I couldn't compute.

It seems important to admit here that this revelation did not happen instantaneously. After all, I am a realist. I am smart and resilient, and I am not the type of person to be bowled over by big emotions—physical pain as a response to emotional turmoil? *Give me a break.* But I must confess that as I slowly embraced this idea, the pain went away altogether. I even canceled a scheduled MRI because I couldn't make it flare over the course of several months. Once I started managing my stress more effectively and talking about my feelings in therapy, the shoulder pain never reappeared. Imagine that.

The patriarch of the mind-body wellness movement is arguably Dr. John Sarno, author of the national bestseller *The Mindbody Prescription: Healing the Body, Healing the Pain*.[1] In the simplest terms, Sarno seeks to help disorders that are "neither illnesses nor diseases, but rather symptomatic states induced by the brain to serve a psychological purpose."[2] These states are those of unwellness, whether that be a stress headache in response to a heavy workload or an unexplained achy throat when we are supposed to perform:

> Conflicts rage constantly in the unconscious, born of the basic elements that represent the mosaic of the human psyche. These conflicts result in the development of emotions that cannot be tolerated and therefore, must be repressed. Because these undesirable feelings appear to strive for recognition, the mind must do something to prevent them from coming to consciousness. Hence the mindbody symptom.[3]

I will ask you to keep an open mind as we study these psychosomatic manifestations. While you may not relate to this discussion, some musicians may, either currently or at some future point in their careers. Many years ago, I taught a young pianist who suffered from debilitating wrist pain. Interestingly, the pain worsened before every performance. While this could be chalked up to increased practice before performances, medical scans and blood work suggested no physical cause. Now many years later, I suspect this was a mind-body symptom of her admittedly severe performance anxiety—her body stepped in to "save" her from the overwhelming threat it perceived.

Psychosomatic pain is very real. While physical causes or explanations may be elusive, the somatic symptoms are decidedly present within the body. Moreover, key features of one's personality predispose them to psychogenic ailments. Perfectionists, highly anxious or fearful people, those who are hostile or volatile, and those who internalize shame or guilt are more likely to experience somatic symptoms of psychological distress.[4] You may have noted the correlation to the enneagram triads; all three drivers of anxiety—shame, fear, and anger—can trigger or exacerbate psychosomatic symptoms. For our purposes in examining performance anxiety, it is important to note that "fear or anxiety can make any symptom worse. This is the one psychogenic process that is generally accepted in medicine."[5]

I can think of no better example of the mind-body connection than performance anxiety. Our mind is integral to this equation: the brain takes in information from the senses and determines that we are under threat. This triggers a cascade of responses—mental, emotional, and physical. We experience intrusive thoughts and scattered focus, and we associate myriad feelings with this state. We also experience very real physical symptoms ranging from shortness of breath, increased pulse, shaky hands, and increased perspiration (to name just a few). Most people accept that mental or emotional stress can cause very real headaches; why are we less inclined to believe that our mental state can impact our physical state in other ways? If this feels like a bridge too far for you, go ahead and skip this chapter. At the very least, the seeds are planted, and you can come back to this discussion later if you need it. If you're ready to consider just how interrelated the body and mind are, and how this can inform your understanding of anxiety, then let's get to it.

## The Mind-Body Approach

The basic tenet of the mind-body connection is that the mind can impact the body in real ways, and too much inner turmoil results in negative physical symptoms. We have all experienced this to some extent. I've already mentioned tension headaches, but we can probably also relate to an upset stomach when nervous, or muscle aches when stressed. I am a fainter, but typically I faint in response to odd physical sensations, not bad news or shocking situations as seen in sitcoms. But a couple years ago, we were suffering through a particularly difficult home move, which required us to undertake extensive repairs. While I was on a trip with the kids, my husband called to deliver some very bad news, and I saw the telltale black clouds in my vision: I was about to faint. My emotional distress resulted in the physical response of fainting—I needed to exit that situation somehow, so my mind and body colluded to ditch consciousness altogether.

Nicole Sachs, creator of the podcast that led me to this concept, explains the mind-body connection in very simple terms, likening it to a well or bucket that is constantly being filled with stressors. The human psyche can withstand quite a lot, but when we reach a critical mass of stress and our bucket is truly full, any additional load will overflow *somewhere*. When mental and emotional stressors can no longer be contained, those stressors seep out into the body and result in physical symptoms. In essence, our brains are trying to get our attention, and they often target bodily areas that we are particularly aware of, such as past points of injury or pain.[6] If we believe that a turn of the weather can impact our bum knee, could we likewise believe that a turn of emotional state could cause it to ache?

Mind-body proponents emphasize that these are universal experiences. We all experience the challenges of the human condition, which include significant mental and emotional stressors. While some may boast a larger stress threshold than others, we all have breaking points. This is one of the key messages of Sarno's work: physical pain due to emotional anguish is universal.[7] It doesn't matter if we think we are not *that* kind of person—the fact that we are human makes us exactly that type of person.

So, what is at the heart of these somatic symptoms? For Sarno, the answer is easy, but it may not be one you expect: rage. For me, the concept of rage was initially uncomfortable and disconcerting, but it came into context the more I studied. Sarno lists potential sources of rage, and the following two may particularly resonate with performers:

- that which results from self-imposed pressure, as in driven, perfectionist, or goodist people
- that which is a reaction to the real pressures of everyday life[8]

He likens the psyche to a bank, suggesting that we make incremental deposits of anger throughout life. When anger reaches a certain threshold and the bank is full, it morphs into rage; when rage is on the brink of eruption, physical symptoms result to keep more detrimental emotional havoc at bay.[9]

You may notice that some of the sources for rage resonate especially with certain enneagram personality types. We know many performers are perfectionists, goodists, and exceptionally driven people—traits reflected in their enneagram types. These traits can foment anger, focused on oneself or others, and it accrues until it reaches a tipping point. We may internalize anger when we are misunderstood or betrayed, or when we cannot execute something perfectly. We may resent others for putting pressure on us or increasing our workload, or we may be frustrated by any number of life's annoyances. Traumas big and small make us rage at our lack of control or autonomy. We may be angered by familial drama or religious contradictions, or we may experience righteous rage at the many, many injustices in our modern world. There is certainly no shortage of causes for anger, and the anger builds incrementally until there is nowhere else for it to go. Many times, we don't even realize this process operating in the background of our consciousness.

There are several exercises for dealing with internalized rage, but in my experience, the most effective is writing down a list of all the current pressures in life, since pressures cause anger. Consider the schedule of a performing arts student: we may be under pressure to complete general education requirements, but frustrated because they take so much time away from music studies. Even music classes require so much work on top of a rigorous production schedule—*do they not know how little time the cast has during tech week?* While we understand that our family cannot travel for the show, our feelings may still be hurt that they can't watch us onstage. We may be jealous of the title role, even if the person cast is a friend. We may feel discouraged and misunderstood when we receive director's notes, or downright mad at drama a castmate causes. We may feel guilty for missing an entrance or embarrassed by a mistake in a dance sequence. All these hypothetical examples circle around just a single week in the life of a performing arts student. Now, extrapolate that to encompass a whole lifetime of human frustrations and traumas. It is easy to see how we internalize remarkable amounts of anger. If this anger isn't dealt with in a way that allows it to effectively "burn out," it will eventually surface in deleterious ways.

I remember reading once that an animal will shake uncontrollably after experiencing trauma. If a rabbit encounters a predator, it will afterward shake for a period of time, literally "shaking it off" as it goes on with life. We may recall a particularly perilous situation, like a terrifying accident or spinning out on ice while driving on the highway. Often, our body takes over. People sometimes urinate from fear, tremble, or cannot control the chattering of their teeth. Our nervous system literally shakes off the adrenaline and completes the full-circle loop that timestamps the end of trauma. With smaller infractions, we don't get that same tidy resolution. Sometimes things that make us angry aren't even rational; our logical self knows that it doesn't make sense to be jealous of a role we could never play, but it doesn't stop the feeling from festering and adding to the heaping pile of anger.

People suffering from low self-esteem are particularly susceptible, as inner feelings of inadequacy can lead to anger and rage often directed at oneself. Likewise, perfectionism is dangerous because perfectionists set unattainable standards and then experience rage and shame when they fail to meet them. Helpers sometimes experience anger at being needed or resent the people they truly do wish to help; they feel taken advantage of, as though they are always expected to step in and do the right thing. Others tend toward anger naturally, like those with volatile tempers. Hostility may sometimes escape in a violent outburst, but these types often suppress excessive amounts of anger in their daily lives. Anytime we feel guilt, sadness, or even dependency on others, it is often tinged with anger, even if we don't realize it.

Anger and other unwanted emotions are, of course, a universal and uncontrollable part of the human experience. Problems arise when our proverbial bucket overflows and our repressed emotions threaten physical or emotional health. Sarno mentions the importance of the Rage/Soothe Ratio, which is exactly what it sounds like—we can engage in self-soothing, which counters rage when it appears in sufficient amounts.[10] It's not hard to list our soothing factors: time with friends, a massage, exercise, drinks with a partner, or a sunny afternoon hike. As long as our soothing factors roughly balance our internalized rage, we will likely fare okay. But, if a hefty stressor tips the scales—a sudden illness, death of a loved one, or serious injury, for example—we are more susceptible to an overflowing well of anger.

This is the most important thing I have learned in my study of the mind-body connection. Without realizing it, I had built many self-soothing mechanisms into my regular life: I know that I need adequate rest and regular massage therapy to keep my body in top performing shape. I also know that I require frequent exercise, prayer, and meditation to maintain my mental and spiritual well-being. I engage in routine therapy to care for my emotional state. I have forged meaningful friendships and know that I am happier when I carve out time with friends. My husband is my soulmate and biggest supporter, and my children bring me great joy (most of the time). All of these are soothing factors for me, and usually they are enough to prevent my bucket from overflowing. I urge everyone to compile a list of soothing factors and be honest about how regularly you engage in things that lessen your emotional load. Are you more inclined to skip some when performance schedules ramp up? (And, is this really in your best interest?)

## Mental Practice and Visualization

I can't remember exactly where I encountered this story, but I recall reading about a professional diver who was injured throughout an entire training season. He practiced mentally while his team practiced physically; every day, he visualized himself hitting the dives perfectly, and he watched videos of the dives on a loop. When he was cleared to resume physical practice, his body was able to accurately execute the dives, even though he had only ever performed them mentally. He had one major advantage over his teammates—he had never practiced the dives wrong, whereas they'd had a season's worth of physical errors in conjunction with accurately executed dives during their practice sessions.

I haven't been able to track down the source of this anecdote, so I can't verify its accuracy. However, I have always been impressed by the efficacy of mental practice and visualization. We have all experienced mental practice, perhaps inadvertently. I once adjudicated a competition in which dozens of candidates submitted recordings of the same piece. I listened to all the highly accurate, polished recordings, and I studied the musical score intently as I did. I contemplated different fingerings for tricky passages, and I considered what I would do differently with articulation or phrasing. When I decided to learn the piece myself years later, I found that my body already knew it pretty well; through my intent mental rehearsal during that judging process, I had internalized the music in a way that surprised me. The same is true when over the course of a show an actor memorizes the entire script, even though they never intentionally practiced castmates' lines. They have mentally rehearsed these lines throughout the production process, and many actors could likely write out the entire show verbatim from simple listening repetition.

I have since read several studies on best practices for visualization and mental rehearsal, and I remain amazed by the results. In short, mental practice is considerably effective when conducted properly. While physical practice remains the gold standard for learning motor skills, we can augment learning by adding mental practice sessions. Ideally, we practice mentally for short blocks of time, only about fifteen seconds long. We choose a very short musical passage (or other physical skill) and repeat that passage several times during the brief timespan. Then, we can choose a new musical excerpt or repeat the same section for another fifteen-second stint. The goal is to accrue entirely accurate repetitions, thereby adding additional successful repetitions on top of those we achieve in physical practice. Research proves that combining mental and physical practice achieves better results.[11] Mental practice is especially important at times when we cannot practice physically due to injury or fatigue, or lack of instrument (like on an airplane flying to auditions). It can also be useful on a performance day when you may not want to practice physically in order to avoid fatigue or last-minute panic when something new goes wrong.

In addition to mental practice, we can visualize positive performing experiences. For instance, I encourage my students to visualize what it will be like when they actually walk onstage. What will they wear, and how will the lights be set? Who will they see in the crowd, and how will they feel about it? When it comes time to take center stage for the actual performance, they have already visualized this situation with a positive outcome. The mind is an incredibly powerful tool that can assist with the speed and quality of physical learning, and in my opinion, mental practice is one of the most underutilized tools for learning.

## Reframing

Visualization can also be exceptionally helpful in reframing memories and the emotions associated with them. Let's return to my opening story from the Prologue. You'll recall that I was invited to my alma mater to play a recital. A major memory slip in the middle caused me to lose focus entirely and complete the performance in a daze, feeling like a fraud and failure. I couldn't understand the compliments afterward, as I grappled with feelings of doubt and shame. Though I didn't realize it at the time, at that moment I was filled with rage. I was mad at myself for "failing," and I was mad at the pressure I perceived from the audience and myself. I felt ashamed for letting people down, and I feared what it meant for my future—would I ever feel confident performing again?

If at that time I had been attuned to the connection between my mind and body, perhaps I could have cut myself some slack. In reality, my bucket was overflowing and had been in overflow mode for some time. In addition to my usual performance anxiety, I had put immense pressure on myself to perform perfectly for my former professors, family, students, and friends. I was exhausted from over-practicing, under-sleeping, and excessive worrying. I had no time for the soothing measures that I might normally engage in—I was fully focused on my performance goal. At the risk of using pregnancy as an easy excuse, I *was* also pregnant and suffering from a weird condition that made my palms and the soles of my feet incredibly itchy, which was infuriating and more than a little distracting for a keyboardist. My husband and I were grappling with abandoning my career to move across the country to be closer to family, and I was terrified that I would be a terrible mother. Furthermore, in an attempt to ensure a healthy pregnancy, I had renounced the eating disorder that had always been my trusty (albeit unhealthy) coping mechanism. Oh, and only Tylenol during pregnancy, so beta-blockers were also out. My bucket was full.

Now that I am convinced of the mind-body connection and understand more fully how my performance anxiety manifests, I am amazed that one little memory slip was *all* that marred that concert. I decided to reframe that difficult moment through visualization. I visualized myself walking onstage and actively tried to experience different emotions than I experienced during the real event. I gave myself time to consider what other emotions may actually have been there, too far under the mountain of stress and anxiety for me to notice. I reframed my nerves as excitement, and instead of looking out into a sea of judgmental faces, I took time to reflect on everyone who had attended. I realized, as I'd probably always known, that they were all there to support me. Many of them *actually loved me*. I mean, my sophomore year math teacher showed up! (I went to a liberal arts college that offered a class called "Mathematical Ideas." We read plays about math, learned the history of Roman numerals, and generally had a pretty fabulous time checking the math gen ed box through a class containing very little actual mathematics.) When I mentally revisit this recital now, instead of feeling petrified and thinking "Ohmygod, Ohmygod, Ohmygod" when I look into the crowd, I experience an overwhelming feeling of support and love. Visualization helped mentally reframe my memory of this event from traumatic to supportive.

## Questions for Reflection

- What are the elements of a performance you can control?
- What are the elements you cannot control?
- Look back on a specific performance and list the things you could control and those you could not. How did each of these affect the final performance?
- Are there any things in your life you try to control, but finally cannot? What would it take to let go of those things and surrender to not being in control of them?
- Make a list of current stressors. Do any of the items cause anger? Can you identify current and/or past sources of internalized rage?
- Have you experienced any physical symptoms of emotional stress?
- What is your current stress threshold? Can you recall a time when you surpassed the threshold? How could you prevent that from happening again?

# Notes

1. John E. Sarno, *The Mindbody Prescription: Healing the Body, Healing the Pain* (New York: Grand Central Life & Style, 1998).

2   Sarno, *The Mindbody Prescription*, 3.
3   Sarno, *The Mindbody Prescription*, xxxviii.
4   Sarno, *The Mindbody Prescription*, 23, 31–2, 42.
5   Sarno, *The Mindbody Prescription*, 42.
6   Sarno, *The Mindbody Prescription*, 143.
7   Sarno, *The Mindbody Prescription*, 8.
8   Sarno, *The Mindbody Prescription*, 11.
9   Sarno, *The Mindbody Prescription*, 12.
10  Sarno, *The Mindbody Prescription*, 29.
11  Kenny, *The Psychology*, 216.

# 9 Why Me?
## Cultural Baggage Impacting Anxiety

I'm grateful never to have struggled with substance addiction. I have deep compassion for those who have, and for those who have suffered abuse and neglect resulting from others' addictions. And yet, eating disorders are essentially addictions—recovery requires dismantling ingrained, hard-learned habits. To that end, I found incredibly meaningful and helpful Laura McKowen's memoir *We Are the Luckiest*, which chronicles her journey to sobriety. While it may seem an even further leap to link performance anxiety with addiction, I would like to remind you of its definition: "Addiction is a compulsive, chronic physiological or psychological need for a habit-forming substance, behavior, or activity involving harmful physical, psychological, or social effects and typically causing well-defined symptoms."[1] Performance anxiety is similarly chronic, involving harmful effects; it certainly causes well-defined symptoms.

Immediately following her memoir's dedication page, McKowen lists nine truths; many of them are particularly apropos to performance anxiety, especially when we find ourselves questioning why we are so afflicted. She begins by reminding us that while it is not our fault, the thing with which we struggle is ultimately our *responsibility*. And, while unfair, McKowen posits, "This will never stop being your thing until you face it." Performance anxiety is our affliction to deal with. It's not fair, but since we know it is our thing, it is ultimately our responsibility—to ourselves, our families, our colleagues, our audiences—to figure out how best to manage it. And, unfortunately, it will *always* be part of us; performance anxiety is a chronic condition that we must continually monitor and treat. Additionally, there are undoubtedly some external pressures—cultural baggage, if you will—that put additional pressure on some groups and personality types.

# Perfection

This year, our family purchased season tickets for our city's NBA team. While I've always been a sports fan, I hadn't lately watched a professional basketball game with such rapt attention. When we went to the season opener, I was aghast: *They miss nearly half the shots they attempt!* We were attending with good friends, and I was seated next to a former band director. I leaned over and shouted to her, "Can you imagine if musicians were so inaccurate? We'd be out of jobs!" She immediately pulled out her phone to show me a piece titled "A+: A Precise Prelude and an Excellent March" by Thomas Duffy. On his website, the composer explains his rationale for this composition, suggesting that in many grading rubrics, an A+ can be awarded even with an error margin of up to 3 percent.[2] We listen to musical recordings that have been edited for complete perfection. We look up to role models who are the very best in their fields, who have reached the pinnacles of their careers; their performances are arguably nearly flawless. Performers simply cannot get by with the same accuracy averages of some other professions (maybe excluding surgeons; let's hope their accuracy is exceptionally high)—even the best NBA players hover around 65 percent shooting accuracy. While I am aware that we certainly cannot compare basketball to music (after all, opponents are not blocking our percussion strikes or stealing our woodwinds), the fact remains that performers are expected to be particularly accurate.

Since an NBA arena didn't exactly allow for good listening to concert band works, I later researched the piece by Duffy and heard recordings. It is not great (by design). Duffy instructs ensemble players to make one planned mistake each; the performers choose whether that mistake will be in note duration, pitch, dynamics, and so on. Barring any other naturally occurring mistakes, this results in a performance that is still roughly 99 percent accurate. Duffy suggests that a performance with a 3 percent error rate, which in academics could still result in an A+, would be nearly unthinkable within the current performing sphere.[3] This piece begs the question of exactly how close to perfection performers are expected to achieve.

We have already discussed perfectionism as a trait of some specific personality types, but it is also a defining characteristic of the performing profession at large. Who would pay hundreds of dollars to see a Broadway show performed at even 90 percent accuracy, with one in every ten notes sung or played incorrectly? The expectation of nearly perfect performances is one of the leading factors contributing to performance anxiety. These very high standards are upheld by the audience members, jury panel, or whomever is observing the performances. Several years ago, GEICO Insurance aired a commercial in which googly eyes pop up everywhere, accompanied by Rockwell's catchy "Somebody's Watching Me." For performers, this is entirely true. We are expected to execute technically demanding musical feats under the critical gaze of others—teachers, audiences, adjudicators, and fans. When we wonder why performers are susceptible to such high rates of anxiety, we must realize that the demands of performing professions are exceptionally high. We do not simply impose perfectionist standards on ourselves. They are real expectations of our profession.

How do we relinquish perfectionism in an industry that demands it? The question is simple, but the answer is incredibly complex and (frustratingly) different for every performer. The first step, of course, is realizing that perfection is an illusion. We must determine what is *good enough* in any particular performing situation: is it enough to maintain good intonation, even if you miss a dynamic shift? Is it enough to execute an aria with musicality and feeling, even if you forget a staging cue? What is acceptable when you are recovering from illness or injury, or haven't slept well all week? If the audience forgives a couple missed notes out of thousands in a Rachmaninoff piano concerto, can you also? What is actually expected of you at this stage in your career?

These questions may seem silly, but for many years I would have answered that only *perfect* would have been *good enough*. I did not understand that if I shot for 100 percent and ended up at 98 percent, that may have been the very best I could attain. I would spend the next week trying to master that elusive 2 percent. I sometimes ask students to write a hierarchy of performance goals for lessons or studio class. The catch is that they cannot choose more than one priority, whether that #1 goal is accuracy, musicality, intonation, memorization, and so on. This exercise stresses that perhaps musicality is more important than accuracy in some passages, or reveals that they need to prioritize memory work in certain spots. However, the larger lesson it teaches is that very often we perform much closer to perfection than to the alternative. Many times, a student will be entirely solid in memorization *and* intonation, even though it ranked lower in their hierarchy; while they may miss a note here or there, accuracy still might be quite high, and the musicality—which perhaps was their #1 goal—came shining through "perfectly." For whatever particular performing situation in which you find yourself, try to ascertain what is truly *good enough*. I will stress that this does not mean lowering standards or expectations. It does mean realistically considering your ability, preparation, career stage, and external circumstances—and, most importantly, adjusting your definition of "perfection" accordingly.

It is challenging not to justify (if only secretly) perfectionism as a positive character trait. I have even touted this "flaw" to my advantage in job interviews: when asked about my weaknesses, I would expel a frustrated sigh, shrug helplessly, and shake my head. In response to the question "What is your biggest weakness?" I would admit that I am, sadly, a perfectionist. *Nothing* is ever good enough for me, diligent and dedicated worker that I am, and I am simply destined to give 110 percent to every endeavor, never satisfied with anything less. Perfectionism, however, wreaks havoc on our emotional, mental, and physical well-being, and it can negatively impact our performance, fomenting a dangerous focus on failure. In addition to fueling anxiety, perfectionism skews our perception, encouraging "a failure (rather than a success) orientation to one's performances."[4]

I mentioned much earlier the Five Stages of Peak Performance presented in *Conquer Anxiety*. One of the most valuable lessons I gleaned from this book was the necessity of mentally moving music from the practice phase to the performance phase.[5] I spent the entirety of my student years (and several years beyond that) perpetually stuck in the practice phase. I practiced up until the very moment I set foot onstage, mentally rehearsing *just one last thing!* I knew deep down that my practicing was never truly done. I sometimes envied other majors whose work was finished when they completed an assignment or read some chapters of a textbook. For me, I knew I could—SHOULD—always eke out just a *little* more practice; when a performance loomed near, I harangued myself for not practicing even more. In reality, most performers know innately when we have completed the practicing phase: when the material is so ingrained that it is part of our very being, when we have put in the hard work and spent hours learning and honing, and when we have checked every box on that practice list, we are ready. Then we must trust our process, our education, and ourselves, and mentally deem the piece performance ready. IT IS ENOUGH.

## Educational Settings and Hierarchical Relationships

When I was in my final semester of doctoral coursework, I decided I could no longer hack it as a musician. My mental health was circling the drain, and I felt absolutely decimated by performance anxiety. The pressures of competition and perfection, whether real or imagined, were more than I could sustain. I continued with applied music lessons, but I dropped all of my required coursework and instead enrolled in Guitar 101 and Creative Nonfiction Writing (still the most fun class I have ever taken, just beating out that undergraduate math class in which we mostly read plays). I wasn't sure what I would do next, but I knew that I could no longer survive as a performer. The demons had won.

During that restless semester, I received a phone call entirely out of the blue, asking me to serve as a sabbatical replacement at the university where I had attained my master's degree. To their knowledge, I was completing doctoral coursework, about to be declared ABD, and in the perfect position to fill in for eight months covering the summer and fall terms. I was flabbergasted. This was my *dream*—I had always wanted to teach college; to be handed the opportunity at an acclaimed music school was beyond my wildest imaginings. I accepted immediately and only later remembered that I had quit music. Eventually, once those eight months were up, I returned to finish my doctorate, knowing that it was the only means to attain my recently codified goal of becoming a music professor.

I often wonder what I would be doing now if I had actually quit; had I not gotten that taste of collegiate teaching, I doubt I would have returned to music. You may recall the statistic from Chapter 1: *20 percent of students who leave music do so because of performance anxiety.*[6] This may not surprise you, especially if you are or have ever been a music student. Students are disproportionately affected by performance anxiety for several reasons. In 1994, Alfred LeBlanc posited a theory about what external pressures cause performance anxiety. Among the pressures, he listed the presence and behavior of an audience, as well as authorities and educators. He also listed family, peer groups, and media as additional stressors in performance settings.[7]

It is not surprising that students are at higher risk for performance anxiety; as a university-level educator, I observe these myriad stressors daily. Students worry not only about their performances, but also about their futures. They fret over how they will survive as artists and where they will end up for further schooling or work. They face incredibly high-pressure situations as they are adjudicated by panels of faculty for examinations and auditions. Students may be living far from family and friends, and they may be adjusting to a new economic situation with financial worries. Often, students' schedules are packed with rehearsals, classes, and performances, in which they likely hold themselves to unattainable standards. Additionally, edited recordings of performers in their prime may further push perfectionism on already stressed students, who may not be equipped with the emotional tools to handle such hefty challenges.[8] In speaking with colleagues, I have found that the ways in which we prepare students for the stage vary wildly. It often depends on a teacher's own experience with performance anxiety: some faculty discuss it routinely, and others rarely or never address the issue.

Not surprisingly, several studies ultimately find that educators and music schools must do more to address student performance anxiety.[9] As we have seen throughout many studies, performance anxiety is in fact an all-too-normalized part of professional musicianship. Educators must study this mental health condition to better serve students. While some students may still abandon their musical dreams due to performance anxiety, at the very least we can identify the problem and provide other options. Perhaps we can serve as the first line of defense for the majority of students who suffer, equipping them with healthy coping mechanisms and strategies to manage anxiety throughout their performing careers.

The student-teacher relationship is particularly precarious. My own musical upbringing is anchored by two exceptional pedagogues who are now close friends and colleagues. These teachers managed to tightrope the fine lines between encouragement and correction, friendship and professionalism. They were kind mentors with unremitting faith in my ability, but they also instructed with decisiveness, constructive criticism, and frank honesty. In my own teaching, I strive to support my students unwaveringly while setting clear boundaries and maintaining attainable high standards. For me, these collaborations exemplify the best of hierarchical relationships, which by definition feature a power imbalance. While the student-teacher relationship is ingrained within performing arts education, it is not the only hierarchical relationship we can imagine: a production director, sports coach, choreographer, ensemble conductor, hiring agent, or even a highly successful peer could assume a hierarchical role within a performer's career.

Such relationships can breed performance anxiety, as performers strive to impress and please those in positions of power. However, these relationships can foment anxiety exponentially if they turn toxic. While I hold the aforementioned professors in the highest esteem, I have also experienced firsthand a much darker realization of the student-teacher relationship. In another academic setting, I endured an abusive professor who wielded full control of the program, exploiting his authority and position. While the sordid details of this inappropriate relationship are perhaps a topic for another, wholly different sort of book, it is enough to say that I felt unsafe and threatened, and there seemed to be nowhere to turn. From my perspective, my future career rested solely within this unpredictable individual's control, and as a powerless student, I found no other recourse.

There is, sadly, no shortage of MeToo narratives, particularly within the performing arts. While I am heartened that offenders are more often being punished for misconduct, there is still much work to be done to prevent these rampant, shameful abuses of power. For the purposes of our discussion, it is enough to say that any type of hierarchical relationship can increase performance anxiety, but particularly unhealthy relationships can cause it to skyrocket. In my case, in addition to my garden-variety performance anxiety, I also feared not knowing what would happen next, how he would respond, what he would require of me, what my peers would think, how I would feel about myself, etc. etc. etc. And sexual misconduct, emotional manipulation, and verbal abuse are not the only hallmarks of toxic hierarchical relationships. Kenny suggests that in worst-case scenarios, instructors can be willfully competitive, volatile, abusive, prejudicial, hurtful, and downright deleterious to their students' progress and personhood.[10]

When a performer experiences excess anxiety due to unhealthy hierarchical relationships, usually the only solution is to cut off the abuser and reclaim autonomy, which can be very difficult—if not impossible—within performing situations. Performers must begin by recognizing the hierarchical relationships within their own performing sphere, which may be myriad. For example, an orchestral instrumentalist may feel subservient to other high-achieving members of the section, the concertmaster, the union leader, the conductor, their own teacher(s)... and the list goes on. These relationships must be further scrutinized to ascertain whether any are causing undue anxiety, and what can potentially be done to mitigate it.

## The Covid-19 Pandemic

As it turns out, experiencing a pandemic can also increase performance anxiety! During the pandemic and beyond, performers were particularly impacted. Theaters were shuttered and concert seasons were suspended; collaboration ground to a halt and recitals took place audience-less, alone in a room via live stream. Ensemble singing and playing ceased, and instruction scurried online, where we learned that certain subjects and instrument types were much less effective via Zoom. An entire planet's worth of performers stopped performing, at least in many traditional ways. We worried about our health, our education, our careers, our finances, and our futures. Some performers explored other career paths and never returned. It is safe to say the performing world has been changed forever, both in negative and positive ways. Perhaps we never appreciated live performance quite as much as when we were forced to abandon it.

The pandemic itself was incredibly stressful, but those stressors did not disappear even as the threats and lockdowns eased. Though much of life may have returned to some semblance of normalcy, "according to the World Health Organization (WHO), since the outbreak of the Covid-19 pandemic, anxiety and depression prevalence increased by 25% globally."[11] While this statistic does not specifically address performance anxiety, we can infer that the performing community as a whole also faced at least a 25 percent escalation in baseline anxiety levels. An increase in general anxiety can lead to increased performance anxiety, so we cannot ignore the lasting impacts of the global pandemic, which have significant bearing on our overall mental well-being.

## Gender and Menopause

Gender is tricky. I am uncomfortable using female/male terminology, as I have had several students and friends for whom that binary does not serve. And yet, there have been several studies on the relationship between gender and anxiety, which I would be remiss not to mention. For the sake of this discussion, I will use the terms "male" and "female," understanding that these labels are oversimplified, unsuitable, and ignore the complexities of many people's lived experiences.

Abrams and Manstead conducted an important study in 1981, in which eighty college students (forty men and forty women) performed in several different situations of varying degrees of pressure (i.e., solo practice versus performing for an audience). Their findings proved that "female participants made fewer performance errors, reported significantly more anxiety than male participants, and attained significantly higher pulse rates than did male subjects."[12] This data was further supported by another study in 1990 (Abel and Larkin) in which college students were monitored before and during semester-end music juries. While both genders reported increased anxiety before the jury, "the female-subject increase was significantly greater than that of the male subjects."[13] A 1997 study out of Michigan State University presented nearly identical findings to the Abrams and Manstead study from sixteen years earlier, noting that music educators must pay particular attention to female students who are disproportionately affected by performance anxiety.[14]

In my own studio, I have found that female students often present with higher levels of performance anxiety than male students. While this could be attributed to several factors, the data supports that females experience markedly higher levels of anxiety than their male counterparts. This predisposition toward increased anxiety is particularly important for female performers to be aware of, especially since mood disorders can be further impacted by hormonal shifts.

Fifty-one percent of the population has ovaries; data suggests that females occupy even a slightly higher percentage of the performing world. While gender is a fluid construct, we are born with physical sex organs, and over half of performers have ovaries and will contend with menopause if they live long enough. Clinically speaking, menopause is achieved after twelve months without a menstrual period, but the symptoms of menopause can persist long after that diagnosis. Likewise, the time of transition into menopause, known as perimenopause, can begin as much as fifteen years prior. Estrogen and progesterone decline during this transition, which can cause new mood disorders and increased anxiety. While we don't often discuss hormonal shifts as catalytic in the performance anxiety equation, many pre-menopausal females understand that low mood, irritability, or anxiety can accompany the estrogen drop preceding regular menstrual cycles (we often refer to this as premenstrual syndrome, or PMS). Imagine these symptoms as a constant state—that is what many women experience during perimenopause and beyond.

As a female performer in my forties, I have begun to study perimenopause and menopause, and I am heartened by the new research and public conversations on this topic—podcast, literary, and social media scenes are exploding with information on menopause, which formerly was a taboo topic shrouded in secrecy. Dr. Mary Claire Haver's 2024 best-selling book *The New Menopause* is one groundbreaking text on this important topic, and she remains at the forefront of menopause advocacy. In large part due to Haver's determined work and that of many other medical professionals like her, at the time I am writing this, America faces progesterone and estradiol shortages; women are finally demanding treatment for their very treatable symptoms. We still know too little and have too few treatment options (especially compared to the extensive research and pharmaceutical interest in male sexual health), but the messages are spreading and women are taking action to ensure their long-term health and well-being.

I remember listening to a podcast on estrogen and its correlation with mental health, and the host dropped a bomb that caused me literally to stop in my tracks (I was running on a treadmill at the time and had to engage the emergency stop mechanism to fully take in what the host was alleging). She noted that among all female age groups, women in perimenopause and menopause suffer from the highest rates of suicide. I was dumbfounded. I don't know what I assumed the most affected age range would be, but it surely wasn't that. After all, we are (rightly) concerned about the mental health of adolescents and teens, who undergo so many social, physical, mental, and emotional changes. I have felt the effects of postpartum depression, and I know firsthand how incredibly hard the child-rearing years are. If anything, I naively assumed women who reach their fifties would be the *happiest*—many would have raised families and be in the golden years of grandparenting, with more time for their own hobbies and needs, or enjoying a well-established career and relationships, right?

I paused the podcast and went immediately to a computer to search JSTOR for some answers (because that is exactly the type of fun-loving person that I am). *Surely the host is mistaken.* She was not mistaken. A 2015 Australian study found the highest suicide rate in women to be among the 45–49 age group, followed closely by those aged 50–54.[15] We have already established that women are more likely than men to experience mental health issues, and these problems intensify during perimenopause and menopause. This is in part due to hormonal changes: both estrogen and progesterone decline during this time, making women vulnerable to mood disruptions and serious mental health disorders. For many women, hormone replacement therapy (HRT) is enough to ease anxiety and keep depression at bay, without the need for other interventions.

I include this section on menopause because I believe it is vitally important for upwards of 51 percent of performers. Since perimenopause can begin for females already in their thirties, a large portion of our performing careers may be impacted by hormonal changes. Especially if we are susceptible to high anxiety, it can worsen during perimenopause and menopause if left untreated. A colleague and I recently discussed this, remarking that it feels like an exceptionally low blow, since many of us feel like we *finally* get a handle on our performance anxiety by this time in our careers. Adding hormonal imbalances to the mix seems cruel and unusual, but it is the reality for performers with ovaries. Finding a provider who will take your unique perimenopause and menopause symptoms seriously, and who will examine HRT options with you, is crucial in managing anxiety for female performers.

## Other Factors

There are any number of additional factors that may add weight to the specific baggage individual performers carry. I had a student in the process of transitioning gender, whose anxiety was increased by worrying about how the audience would perceive their changing looks and voice. I taught an international student who suffered from extreme depression and anxiety, who was in the United States simply because her family believed an American university degree to be the pinnacle of success. She struggled with perfectionism and ultimately quit music altogether, unable to endure the impossible load. Performers may face the pressure of proving themselves to a financial benefactor or bear the burden of a particular type of political or religious upbringing. Once in my office, a student buried her face in her hands the day of her graduate recital, saying, "Oh my God, I am so SCARED for tonight!" I assured her that she was ready and would be fabulous, and she laughed, "Oh, I'm not that nervous to perform. I'm scared that my mom and dad are going to hear me sing about sex! They're super conservative." The list of performance anxiety-inducing triggers is unending, and we need to carefully consider what our personal baggage includes, and exactly how much it is pouring into our proverbial buckets.

## *Questions for Reflection*

- Make a list of all the contributing factors for your performance anxiety. What is the cultural baggage you carry?
- Do you struggle with perfectionism? What percentage would actually be *good enough*? Does this vary for recordings, live performances, lessons, and so on?
- If you are a mentor to other performers (or may be in the future), how can you be mindful of their unique cultural baggage?
- Speak with some close friends about the factors contributing to their performance anxiety. What are the common issues you all face? What is different?
- How might you begin to lessen your personal load of cultural baggage? Do you require outside help or support?

## Notes

1   *Merriam-Webster*, s.v. "addiction," https://www.merriam-webster.com/dictionary/addiction (accessed April 6, 2024).

2. Thomas Duffy, *A+: A Precise Prelude and an Excellent March*, https://www.duffymusic.com/a-a-precise-prelude-and-an-excellent-march.html (accessed March 5, 2024).

3. Duffy, *A+: A Precise Prelude and an Excellent March*.

4. Kenny, *The Psychology*, 75.

5. Skidmore, Shallenberger, and Shallenberger, *Conquer Anxiety*, 109.

6. Gómez-López and Sánchez-Cabrero, "Current Trends in Music Performance Anxiety Intervention."

7. Albert LeBlanc, "A Theory of Music Performance Anxiety," *The Quarterly* 5, no. 4 (Winter 1994): 60–8.

8. Gómez-López and Sánchez-Cabrero, "Current Trends in Music Performance Anxiety Intervention."

9. Gómez-López and Sánchez-Cabrero, "Current Trends in Music Performance Anxiety Intervention."

10. Kenny, *The Psychology*, 288.

11. World Health Organization, "COVAX Delivers Its 1 Billionth Covid Vaccine Dose/Covid-19 Pandemic Triggers 25% Increase in Prevalence of Anxiety and Depression Worldwide," *Saudi Medical Journal* 43, no. 4 (2022), https://www.who.int/news/item/02-03-2022-covid-19-pandemic-triggers-25-increase-in-prevalence-of-anxiety-and-depression-worldwide (accessed March 5, 2024).

12. Albert LeBlanc, Young Chang Jin, Mary Obert, and Carolyn Siivola, "Effect of Audience on Music Performance Anxiety," *Journal of Research in Music Education* 45, no. 3 (Autumn 1997): 482.

13. LeBlanc et al., "Effect of Audience on Music Performance Anxiety," 482.

14. LeBlanc et al., "Effect of Audience on Music Performance Anxiety."

15. Jayashri Kulkarni, "Perimenopausal Depression—an Under-recognised Entity," *Australian Prescriber* 41, no. 6 (December 2018): 183.

# 10 Assembling the Toolkit
*Preparation and Performance*

Aside from medication options, the next question I most often receive from students is how I personally practice and prepare for performance. The teacher in me loves this question: *Compare and contrast your preparation and performance regimens before and after your study of performance anxiety.* Happily! Thank you for asking! I know a lot more about myself as a person and performer, having undertaken this large-scale self-study. If I were to teach a course on performance and all it entails, it would conclude with this information. Here are the tricks in my toolkit and how I have assembled it, given the research I have done on my personality and my particular brand of performance anxiety.

## Energy

As an enneagram type 3 (Achiever), I have a lot of energy; I have excess amounts of energy surrounding performances. My adrenaline runs high, and I note an increased heart rate already several days before a performance. You may have experienced this as well—you usually sit through recitals as a typical audience member, enjoying the concert. But when your own recital looms near, you may feel increased anxiety while listening to someone else's performance; sometimes I find myself holding my breath while others perform. I need to physically burn off energy, so I schedule lots of exercise into my performing weeks, and I don't "take it easy" (as some teachers encouraged me to do). For me, sprints and other high-intensity interval training (HIIT) burn off the most excess energy, and I engage in those activities several times a week leading up to a performance.

As we discussed in the several chapters focused on the enneagram, each type has differing amounts of energy specific to their personality. What works for me will not work for everyone. For example, lower energy groups need to conserve energy or work through calming movements like yoga. During my early musical training, several very well-meaning teachers intimated that my favored activities were inappropriate for a performance week. They suggested lower-impact sports or perhaps a brisk walk around the neighborhood. While I appreciate their good intentions, I now suspect they were not enneagram types with high-energy reserves. I know myself intimately, and I know that energy accumulates in me until I literally feel like my chest will explode and steam will come rolling out of my ears. That is how I feel during a *normal* week. When I experience higher-than-usual amounts of adrenaline flooding my system, my body needs additional physical outlets.

It took me a long time to accept this truth. I used to give the same advice I had received to my own students: *Take it easy. Get lots of rest and save up your energy for your recital day!* I had internalized the message so thoroughly: what my body craved was wrong. I was a fool to run sprints the morning of a recital—what if I got hurt? I would exercise in secret, as though committing a heinous crime—a clandestine jump squat here, a covert push-up there. A few years ago, my doctoral teacher, who is now a dear friend and letter-writing pen pal, gave me a green light with a cavalier, "Honey, do whatever the hell you want to do! You've earned it." And so, I began to do whatever my body wanted on performance days. Through trial and error, I became wiser—I don't lift heavy weights on performance days because that strains my fingers. I run sprints on the treadmill to avoid rolling an ankle on uneven asphalt outside, and I lower the speed a little to prevent injury or exhaustion. But exercise is an integral part of my performance preparation, especially on concert days.

I encourage students to assess their own energy levels. For those with measured energy reserves, like Investigators (type 5), I encourage tracking every energy output on their calendar for a performance day. Perhaps it's not a good idea for them to have breakfast with visiting family or play in a friend's recital the night before; for them, every interaction is a withdrawal from their energy bank. Because I know that Fives have only a certain amount of energy each day, which cannot be increased, I know that unlike me, they actually do need to conserve their energy for an evening performance. Those students may need to take a walk, drink some tea, meditate, and take a bubble bath before they are ready to go onstage that night.

# Confession #3

Up until this point, I have neglected to reveal that I am an organist. I have referred to myself and my students as keyboardists; that is true, but I specialize in organ. Full confession: I chose this true-but-not-the-whole-truth terminology in part because I wanted to build rapport without minds wandering to any preconceived notions anyone may have about organists. *What stereotypes would those be*, you ask? Well, in an effort not to offend colleagues or students, I shall simply say that I very frequently hear, "You just don't strike me as an organist!" It seems folks intend that as a compliment, so it stands to reason that some people harbor somewhat ungenerous ideas about the type of person who plays my instrument. Furthermore, the organ is admittedly a niche specialty within the performing world, and I hoped this discussion could be broader.

# Logging Mistakes

Stereotypes aside, I want to use organ playing as an example of full-body movement requiring exceptional proprioceptive and kinesthetic skills (what, you don't think of organists as naturally athletic?). The organ requires all four limbs working simultaneously with great accuracy and dexterity, so organists must constantly be aware of their entire bodies as they play. We have not yet discussed the ins and outs of physical practice, but that of course is the main activity in performance preparation. Everyone has different practice requirements, and some instruments have clear physical thresholds: a vocalist cannot sing for eight hours straight, nor will a horn player's lips withstand the same amount of continuous rehearsal. For musicians, the amount and sort of practice you do are determined by your instrument, your body, your instruction, and your individual practice needs. Nonetheless, I have found that certain practice techniques can help combat performance anxiety—my favorite is logging mistakes.

I often tell students that we rarely make stupid mistakes. By the time students study collegiately, it is much more likely that errors result from kinesthetic miscalculations—at least on my instrument. I have found that an easy way to take control of mistakes is to actually log these mistakes, along with the reason for making them. Nine times out of ten, we can discover a definitive reason for the mistake. In early study, I often suggest that students fill in a very simple error log, which we will examine shortly.

I also encourage tracking physical tendencies and sensations during performance. We know our bodies gravitate to the fetal position in times of great stress—we curl inward toward a sense of security, tightening into a ball to protect our vital organs and take up less space. In musical performance, organists tend toward this same posturing—elbows skewing inward toward the torso, and feet pulling back toward the body. As you can imagine, these slight physical alterations can be monumentally detrimental. Noticing that the left knee is rotated slightly inward and causing undershooting of an interval is paramount to fixing the problem; knowing that it is more likely to happen in performance when the body tends to contract due to nerves is also crucial. Here is a sample of an error log, showing the error and the resolution: (See Table 10.1)

Table 10.1 *Error Log Documenting Occurrences, Causes, and Solutions for Mistakes*

| Date | Piece | Measure or Location of Error | Error | Cause | Resolved |
|---|---|---|---|---|---|
| 2/27 | Bach E-flat M prelude | m. 18, pedal | ascending seventh was wrong, played sixth | right knee was too far in | YES—brought right knee back out |
| 2/27 | Demessieux "O Filii" | third system, fourth measure, right hand | last note wrong: playing second instead of third | fingers want to play same pattern as previous measure, which is stepwise | YES—marked skip in score and changed fingering |
| 2/28 | Franck "Pièce Héroïque" | page 3, second system arpeggios | inaccurate AM arpeggio in LH, keep hitting wrong notes | wrist position? | NO |

Simply being able to identify physical causes for mistakes allows students to take real control and fix them in the future. If a student cannot identify the problem or cannot resolve the error in private practice (like in the third example above), then we will examine solutions in lessons. Often, as an observer, I am able to see kinesthetic pitfalls that the student cannot.

While these sorts of physical mistakes often cause instrumentalists' errors, it is important to note that not all mistakes stem from physical miscalculations. Many of my colleagues in voice and brass areas, for example, note that errors on their instruments are often caused by mental mistakes or lapses. Each performer needs to determine their own process for error identification and correction. However, I believe that acknowledging errors and creating a plan for their remediation is essential for all performers during the practicing phase.

I am amazed at how often students simply start a piece or passage over and hope for a better outcome without examining the root causes of the mistakes—sometimes they don't even know what mistake they made, just that "it was wrong." I frequently say in lessons that knowing is more than half the battle: if we don't know what went wrong, we simply cannot trust that we have fixed it. Before a performance, students can look back through their error log and prove that they have in fact worked out many problems and arrived at real solutions. Once this process becomes habitual, performers can internalize error detection and resolution and may stop writing out physical logs. If accuracy continues to be a challenge, then we will consider auxiliary practice methods like visualization and mental rehearsal.

## Mental Preparation

In earlier chapters, I mentioned my love of fiction. While reading books may seem a frivolous use of time when preparing for a performance, I find it vital for my mental well-being. Reading provides a release for me, a welcome respite from reality. Whether one enjoys reading or not, an escape mechanism is crucial. This can be carving out time to watch a film or play a video game, or simply taking a walk outside and enjoying the weather.

I also engage in mental practice leading up to performances, which I find becomes especially important the better I know my repertoire. At a certain point in the practice process, physical repetition becomes somewhat redundant.

While it is nevertheless important, it can be challenging to truly engage in meaningful rehearsal, rather than just utilizing muscle memory and mindlessly "going through the motions." I encourage my students to focus on new parts of the music—playing the piece concentrating mostly on a counter-melody, or the specific release of notes, or using rhythmic subdivisions to assess accurate durations. At this polishing stage, mental rehearsal is an invaluable tool; plus, it adds to the number of accurate repetitions a performer has been able to accomplish through physical practice.

Perhaps most importantly, I carve out time to visualize my entire performance. Since visualization and mental practice have been proven to occur in the brain in real time, this exercise should take approximately as long as the entire concert will take to perform. On a day that I am well-rested, I sit down for a full hour (or longer) and visualize every step of the performance process: what I will wear, how the lighting will be, how the applause will sound. Then, I go through my concert in order, mentally rehearsing the music while visualizing myself from above or behind, sitting at the organ. Some of my students find this process so helpful and comforting that they do it multiple times during a recital week. One student told me it felt like being able to see into the future, and that he encountered an odd sense of dèjá vu when he actually played his recital, having visualized it so many times.

As I mentioned earlier, the importance of sleep cannot be overstated. I try to get good sleep before a performance, though that is not always possible with the rigors of work and the responsibilities of life (or while raising small children). Because I know my mental health is more grounded when I engage in therapy and massage, I try to schedule a massage in the days leading up to an important performance; likewise, I plan a therapy session around the date. Because I also understand the mind-body connection and how and why my personal bucket overflows, I try to avoid other stressors to the best of my ability. Life is messy, and we cannot always ensure stress-free days leading up to performance. But we can do our best to bolster the framework that supports our mental, emotional, and physical health.

## The Physiological Sigh

I learned about the physiological sigh from the *Huberman Lab* podcast, and I have since implemented it for help with anxiety; it is particularly useful right before going onstage and even during performance. It is a real-time tool that immediately calms the nervous system and slows heart rate. Huberman notes that there is "a way in which you can breathe that directly controls your heart rate through the interactions between the sympathetic and the parasympathetic nervous system."[1] Based on the movement of the diaphragm, the heart either expands or contracts, forcing more or less blood to pump through it. This in turn determines whether the heart rate will slow down or speed up. Exhale-focused breathing causes the heart to slow down, thereby calming the nervous system. The physiological sigh is an intentional breathing pattern of two quick inhales followed by one long exhale; you can repeat this pattern as long as you wish (or as long as you're able within a performance). Huberman emphasizes that the physiological sigh is "the tool that is the fastest—and most thoroughly grounded in physiology and neuroscience—for calming down in a self-directed way."[2] It's easy to prove this works. Anyone with a heart rate-tracking watch can actually observe the beats per minute decrease while engaging in this breathing method.

One way to practice this sort of self-calming is to replicate a stressful situation and actively work on raising your stress threshold. Since performance anxiety is a response to increased adrenaline, I often encourage students to find ways to elevate their heart rate in practice sessions when they are not otherwise agitated. A quick burst of jump squats, a sprint around the building, or several jumping jacks will usually do the trick (as long as they are physically able to sustain this sort of exercise). This results in similar physical symptoms to performance anxiety—instant perspiration, shortness of breath, increased heart rate, shaky hands. The student then works on self-calming, using the physiological sigh or other techniques. We are able to increase the stress threshold through increased exposure, and this also builds trust in our ability to calm our nervous system in real time.

As a member of the so-called Anxiety (Feeling) Triad, I use the physiological sigh constantly. Often, my anxiety sparks at random moments throughout the day; sometimes I find myself holding my breath for no apparent reason. The physiological sigh occurs naturally in people and animals before drifting off to sleep—you may be able to envision your family dog giving a deep sigh before curling up to rest. I often check my heart rate on my watch, and I use this tool anytime I find my pulse higher than usual. It is particularly helpful when performances approach, and I use this breathing pattern even during concerts. It often helps to associate the physiological sigh with applause, engaging this tool with every bow, or a pause between production numbers, or while switching out music on the stand.

## Interrupters

Even with the best preparation, performance anxiety still creeps in. Sometimes, we can anticipate its approach; other times, it swoops in deftly when we least expect it. The good news is that performers can utilize tools like the physiological sigh to mitigate anxiety in real time when it occurs; I call these "interrupters." Performance anxiety exists in a loop, a vicious cycle in which thoughts fuel anxiety, which in turn activates more negative thoughts. During performance, it is crucial to have interrupters on hand to arrest the snowballing of performance anxiety.

Some performers gravitate to grounding techniques, focusing on things they can see, hear, taste, smell, or touch. During my undergraduate days, I realized I needed something to quickly bring me back into my body when I felt anxiety escalating and pulling me into a mental frenzy. I adopted a habit of ticking my tongue against the roof of my mouth, creating a barely audible metronomic click with the pulse of whatever music I was playing. This simple physical gesture remains my go-to interrupter, a physical task enacted when I feel anxiety take hold. A vocalist colleague told me she taps her pinky finger against the back of her leg during performance, which helps ground her. Many instrumentalists intuitively tap their toes during performance, but they must formulate a different, distinct gesture to serve as an interrupter. A student cellist told me he actively presses his non-dominant leg into the chair as a grounding mechanism, and a singer reported scanning the audience for a specific color.

One of my favorite interrupters is humming. I often encourage students to hum at the keyboard, either along with the music they are playing or in monotone. While many performers use their mouths and/or voices and therefore cannot hum while performing, they might find a quick moment during applause or backstage before the show. A recent 2023 study proves that humming "can help enhance the parasympathetic nervous system and slow down sympathetic activation."[3] Humming serves as a sort of active meditative practice, and it is a powerful interrupter when performance anxiety strikes.

## Motivation, Medication, and Meditation

I recall many times before recitals trembling in a green room, nervously checking my watch seven hundred times, pacing until the minute I was called to the stage. I would feign coolness, laughing with the crew backstage, pretending it was no big deal: *Oh, sure, whatever you want to do! I'll just walk on whatever way you want—it doesn't matter to me!* I didn't want to be rude, and I didn't want to appear a nervous wreck, so I would never dare ask them to leave me alone and cut the chit-chat, or sit in a dark corner with my eyes closed to focus. I would just pop a beta-blocker or two and go onstage hoping that it would go well.

My pre-game ritual is quite different now that I have discovered what I really require to perform well and understand my performance anxiety on a much deeper level. Pre-performance rituals are particularly important and consistently prove effective. In a 2008 study of athletes (Lonsdale and Tam),[4] researchers documented pre-performance rituals for each player: "Results showed that players were more successful when they followed their dominant behavioral sequence (84% success) than when they deviated from a specific behavioral pattern (71% success)."[5] You might be able to envision your favorite basketball player and exactly what they do before shooting a free throw, or note the way a pro golfer readies for a swing.

The time right before a performance has become sacred for me; I actually look forward to it. I begin by sitting quietly and assigning my dedications. I think carefully about each piece and what I have experienced during the learning process of that particular work. Then, I mentally dedicate the piece to someone—a friend, family member, colleague, or other loved one. These people will never know about the dedications, but it allows me to assign meaning to the musical pieces in a fresh way; moreover, concentrating on a person who means a lot to me takes away a modicum of the anxiety I feel while performing. I try not to form opinions and ideas about these dedications during my practice—this is a special thing I save just for performance.

Because through trial and error I have learned exactly how much medication I need to quell the somatic symptoms of my performance anxiety, I take 20 mg of propranolol (a non-selective beta-blocker, as you'll recall) about forty-five minutes pre-performance. I take an additional 10 mg thirty minutes later, which I dissolve under my tongue, mostly because it makes me feel a little rebellious. I use the physiological sigh when I feel my heart rate rising, and sometimes I observe it slowing while monitoring it on my watch. Knowing I can control my heart rate through the physiological sigh is empowering, and I appreciate the reminder right before performing.

Then, in whatever time I have left before curtain, I meditate. Sometimes, I use prayer beads to help guide my racing mind. I practice controlled, exhale-focused breathing, keeping my eyes closed. Over the course of the meditation, I remind myself of the positive aspects of my personality—hard work, determination, and the high standards of my Achiever type have gotten me to this point. I also remind myself of the work I have done to balance the pitfalls of my enneagram type: I cannot outrun my anxiety, but I do have the power to mitigate it. I remind myself that my work is in the performance stage; I have fought the good fight in the practice rooms, and now I am fully prepared and able to perform.

## *A Note for Performers of Other Enneagram Types*

The process outlined above works well for me, an enneagram type 3 (Achiever) and member of the Feeling Triad (types 2, 3, and 4), but each performer must assemble their own individualized toolkit for practice and performance. For example, a performer within the Thinking Triad (types 5, 6, and 7) may be well served by creating a practice chart containing concrete time blocks and practice assignments in order to combat procrastination and indecision. They might need to conserve energy pre-performance and consult their Courage Log or physical success symbols before going onstage. A performer belonging to the Doing Triad (types 8, 9, and 1) may have excess energy leading up to performance, which they might burn off through physical exercise. These types could benefit in the practice phase by creating a list of current pressures and wrongs and defusing any resulting anger they feel. The specific tricks, tips, and work suggested for each type are contained in the chapters on the enneagram and its triads, and each performer must engage in mindful trial and error to discover which tools work best for them.

## Questions for Reflection

- What has been your performance preparation regimen in the past? Has this changed over time?
- What advice have you received from teachers or colleagues regarding performance preparation? Has it helped you?
- Is there any part of your preparation that could be more streamlined or systematized? Could a practice log help focus your attention?
- Create a timeline for your ideal concert day. What would it include? What would it exclude?
- Even when you cannot attain a perfect performance day, what are the non-negotiable elements you must retain to do your best?
- Are there any things you could consider adding to your performance preparation toolkit?

## Notes

1. Andrew Huberman, "Tools for Managing Stress and Anxiety," episode 10, March 8, 2021, *Huberman Lab*, Scicomm Media, https://www.hubermanlab.com/episode/tools-for-managing-stress-and-anxiety (accessed February 27, 2024), 23:30.
2. *Huberman Lab*, "Tools," 21:31.
3. Gunjan Trivedi, Kamal Sharma, Banshi Saboo, Soundappan Kathirvel, Ashwati Konat, Vatsal Zapadia, Poonjan J. Prajapati, Urva Benani, Kahan Patel, and Suchi Shah, "Humming (Simple Bhramari Pranayama) as a Stress Buster: A Holter-Based Study to Analyze Heart Rate Variability (HRV) Parameters During Bhramari, Physical Activity, Emotional Stress, and Sleep," *Cureus* 15, no. 4 (2023): e37527. https://doi.org/10.7759/cureus.37527.
4. C. Lonsdale and J. T. Tam, "On the Temporal and Behavioural Consistency of Pre-Performance Routines: An Intra-Individual Analysis of Elite Basketball Players' Free Throw Shooting Accuracy," *Journal of Sports Sciences* 26, no. 3 (2008): 259–266.
5. Kenny, *The Psychology*, 212.

# Epilogue
## *It's Still Complicated*

I recently performed an exceptionally meaningful recital. I was invited to play a solo concert for a convention of the foremost professional organization for my instrument. I was honored (and scared), and I knew immediately what I wanted to present: a rarely performed, large-scale, sixty-five-minute piece for organ, alternating with narration. My former undergraduate professor, Lorraine, who is a very close friend and excellent public speaker, agreed to narrate. I have never before experienced such compelling motivation to perform. I adored the relatively unknown piece and simply could not wait for others to experience it. I was performing with a dear friend and mentor, and the packed hall was full of eager colleagues, former and present students, friends, and family who truly wanted to be there.

I engaged in all the steps outlined in the previous chapter. I had dominated my preparation process. I just *knew* the concert was going to be wildly successful. Indeed, the first two movements (of fourteen) went off without a hitch. I felt only mildly nervous. I remember thinking, "This is going so well!" And then it happened—a cipher. For organists, this is one of the worst instrument malfunctions that can occur. Basically, it means that a specific pipe continuously receives the signal to sound, and it cannot be shut off. It creates a constant drone, and the player is left simply to hope and pray that it will disappear. Luckily, the pipe was a relatively low, quiet tone, and audience members later reported barely noticing it. Up at the instrument, however, it was a deafening roar. I locked eyes with Lorraine, and we exchanged an imperceptible nod: *the show must go on.*

The performance *was* wildly successful. The audience loved the work, and I played exceptionally well. Except, I hadn't noticed. It took every ounce of my mental stamina to keep playing against that monumental distraction. I relied on muscle memory and sheer nerve to power through the remaining twelve movements. When I released the final notes, I felt an immediate, immense migraine take root; I tasted iron. My body felt like rubber, as though I'd run a marathon. Colleagues rushed up to congratulate me, and I could barely craft intelligible responses. Lorraine wrapped me in a huge hug and repeated what she'd said a decade earlier, in that much different performance situation: "You handled it like a pro!" This time, I believed her.

Even when we are fully prepared and mentally fortified, live performance is still live performance—*anything* can happen. In the end, performing takes resilience, nerve, and grit. We keep performing for a reason, though that reason differs for all of us. Many times, we succeed wildly; sometimes, we do not. As Angela Duckworth writes in *Grit: The Power of Passion and Perseverance*:

> To be gritty is to keep putting one foot in front of the other. To be gritty is to hold fast to an interesting and purposeful goal. To be gritty is to invest, day after week after year, in challenging practice. To be gritty is to fall down seven times, and rise eight.[1]

We foster grit, resilience, and nerve through daily practice. The ideas and exercises in this book are designed to help you identify the work you must do to cultivate it; that work is different for every single performer. All performers must understand how performance anxiety is triggered by the brain, and how they specifically respond to the increased adrenaline that incites the evolutionary fight-or-flight response. Resilience can be bolstered by turning down the volume of somatic symptoms. Personally, beta-blockers slow my heart rate and diminish the perspiration on my hands, and the mitigation of those hugely distracting physical symptoms quells performance anxiety substantially. The physiological sigh works in real time to slow heart rate and calm the nervous system.

Building grit, or nerve, also involves a good deal of emotional and mental work. As performers, we are accustomed to the immense amounts of physical practice required to perform. However, we often ignore the emotional and mental practices also required. The enneagram triads reflexively tend toward three very different emotional responses: the Feeling Triad to shame, the Thinking Triad to fear, and the Doing Triad to anger. I believe these emotions are the drivers of performance anxiety in each triad, and our work of managing these emotions is lifelong. Nevertheless, this work is exceptionally effective, particularly when paired with clinical psychotherapy. Practical exercises like Courage and Fear Logs, practice journals, and meditative endeavors can help keep shame, fear, and anger within manageable ranges.

Performers must also be aware of the mind-body connection, particularly when the stressors of life accumulate. While not all performers will experience psychogenic pain, all performers possess a breaking point. Our reservoir for hurt, rage, shame, fear, and all the other dark emotions can only contain so much before it overflows and impacts body, mind, and performance. Mental practice, visualization, and reframing all take place within the mind; its potential for learning and adapting is amazing and cannot be overstated. Likewise, the power of the heart is immense; determining meaningful motivation for performing is equally essential.

One of the key truths I've learned through decades of performing and teaching is that each performer is wholly unique. While we all may fit more or less within the nine enneagram types, our past traumas, cultural baggage, stress thresholds, and lived experiences are entirely personal. Certain performers are predisposed to higher levels of performance anxiety, due both to nature and nurture. But, while our first response may reflexively be shame, fear, or anger, we possess the power to truly control our *second* response. This book is designed to cultivate healthier, more courageous second responses.

Performance anxiety is at best a frustrating annoyance, and at worst a debilitating, life-threatening ailment. It attacks confidence and self-worth, and it can cost dearly. In *The Psychology of Music Performance Anxiety*, Kenny studies musicians with extreme performance anxiety, part of the subgroup she defines as those "whose experience of anxiety is so pervasive and profound that it is experienced as a defining characteristic of their sense of self."[2] Sadly, some high-anxiety musicians present with suicidal ideations; Kenny reports several highly successful musicians who admit to unbearable feelings of worthlessness, shame, and intense fear. These musicians self-reported suicidal feelings and thoughts directly resulting from their performance anxiety.[3] While many performers suffer milder levels of anxiety, these case studies illuminate how utterly devastating and destructive performance anxiety can be.

Brené Brown sheds some light on the prevalence of anxiety, proving yet again that we are not alone:

Approximately one third of U.S. adults will be affected by an anxiety disorder in their lifetime; however, it is estimated that fewer than half of people with diagnosable anxiety seek any type of professional treatment. It's very difficult to work through an anxiety disorder without professional help.[4]

Statistically, you know someone—likely multiple people—suffering from an anxiety disorder. Chances are good that person may be you, your students, your colleagues, or your friends and family members. You will recall that the American Psychological Association classifies performance anxiety as a subset of social anxiety disorder. Professional help, whether therapy, medication, HRT, or some other form, is available, and more importantly, it is *effective*. It is a travesty that not even half of anxiety sufferers find, or even seek, the professional assistance they need. This is a statistic in drastic need of change, and it is up to us to effect it.

In 2018, Brené Brown introduced the term "grounded confidence" in her acclaimed book *Dare to Lead*. She explains, "It's not fear that gets in the way of courage, it's armor—how we self-protect when we feel uncertain or fearful."[5] She suggests that grounded confidence is a continual quest in which we slowly dismantle that armor through curiosity and intentional discovery about ourselves. As performers, our armor attempts to protect us from shame, fear, and anger, but it actually keeps us from realizing our fully potentiated selves. These emotions threaten self-worth, which is the very key to developing grounded confidence. On the other hand, self-discovery and continual learning about our unique approaches to the world and relationships with performance will nurture confidence based on an unshakable knowledge of our inherent worth.

Sometimes we refer to particularly harrowing or stressful events as "unnerving." Merriam-Webster defines that to "unnerve" is "to deprive of courage, strength, or steadiness."[6] *That* is what performance anxiety does—it robs us of the courage, strength, and steadiness that we painstakingly cultivate through endless hours of practice, rehearsal, and preparation. Only by more fully understanding yourself and exactly what drives your performance anxiety can you reclaim that nerve—through honesty, courage, determination, and transformative, intentional work. Performance anxiety will ebb and flow throughout a lifetime of performance, but one thing will remain certain: your potential is limitless. The past many pages are filled with suggestions, practices, and assignments for realizing full performing potential, replete with a healthy, immutable, unshakable dose of nerve. The journey will be long and winding, and the work will be substantial and arduous at times. Nevertheless, I promise it is worth it. *You* are worth it.

## Notes

1. Angela Duckworth, *Grit: The Power of Passion and Perseverance* (New York: Scribner, 2016), 275.
2. Kenny, *The Psychology*, 261.
3. Kenny, *The Psychology*, 250.
4. Brown, *Atlas* 10.
5. Brown, *Atlas*, 254.
6. *Merriam-Webster*, s.v. "unnerving," https://www.merriam-webster.com/dictionary/unnerving (accessed March 14, 2024).

# Acknowledgments

I am indebted to very many who made sharing this work possible. To Michael Tan, Acquisitions Editor for Music at Rowman and Littlefield, I am forever grateful for your interest in this topic and for your attentive assistance from proposal through publication. To my editor Danielle Kutner, thank you for examining every character of my manuscript and teasing out its finest version. I am grateful for the brilliant cover art created by Stefan Prodanovic; he took my wildest imaginations and gave them form. Thank you to illustrator Sara Ángel, whose work allows us to understand the brain in a more tangible way, and to Joanna Smolko for her deft indexing. To everyone at Bloomsbury, I am tremendously grateful for your tireless work in bringing *Unnerved* to life.

This book began as a niggling idea, which I discussed in passing with my very close friend and mentor Lorraine Brugh. She proffered heartfelt encouragement, and when I began to furiously write these ideas, Lorraine received them with her trademark curiosity. She read and edited each chapter judiciously; this book—and my life—is infinitely better for her involvement. Lorraine passed away unexpectedly in January 2025, just before I'd received the news that Bloomsbury was considering *Unnerved* for publication. Throughout the final editing and publication process, I have felt her loss keenly. I miss my sounding board, cheerleader, mentor, proofreader, and most of all, my very dear friend. This book exists in large part because of Lorraine. She appears in the Prologue and reappears in the Epilogue, and her presence lingers on every page in between. I am the performer and person I am today thanks to Lorraine's tutelage, friendship, and love. I dedicate this book to her memory.

Through its many iterations, *Unnerved* took form thanks to the input, suggestions, critique, and wisdom of many friends. To my closest friend and the most brilliant person I know, Christina Wallace: thank you for your unwavering support and encouragement. Elizabeth Bard provided invaluable insight into brain science and therapy modalities, and I am grateful for her loving friendship and kindness every day. I owe particular thanks to Laura Ketchum for her immediate willingness to read my manuscript at several key stages. Laura is a fierce friend and one of the smartest and most generous people I know. Several colleagues and former students gave freely of their time and opinions to help with this project. I am indebted to everyone who read portions and considered how I could improve this work and make it more relevant and accessible.

Finally, I'd like to express my humble and enduring gratitude to my husband and soulmate Ryan Williams. I knew he was The One the moment he smiled, waved, and ambled in my direction on our very first date, nearly twenty years ago. He remains my one-and-only, and I cannot imagine life without his steady, faithful presence. Ryan is the hardest worker I have ever met, and he inspires me endlessly. He is my truest critic, biggest supporter, and best friend; our beautiful life is my proudest work. To Charlie and Maddie, our amazing, brilliant children: you have changed my life in the most remarkable ways, and you make me a better person each and every day. I love you to the moon and back, "kinfinity," permanent marker.

# References

Ackerman, Sandra. *Discovering the Brain*. Washington, DC: National Academy Press, 1992.

American Psychological Association. "Cognitive Processing Therapy." July 31, 2017. https://www.apa.org/ptsd-guideline/treatments/cognitive-processing-therapy (accessed March 19, 2025).

Bourgeois, James A. "The Management of Performance Anxiety with Beta-Adrenergic Blocking Agents." *Jefferson Journal of Psychiatry* 9, no. 2 (June 1991): 13–28.

Brown, Brené. *Atlas of the Heart*. New York: Random House, 2021.

Brown, Brené. *I Thought it was Just Me (But it Isn't): Making the Journey from "What Will People Think" to "I Am Enough"*. New York: Avery, 2007.

Chang, Joanne C., Elizabeth Midlarsky, and Peter Lin. "Effects of Meditation on Music Performance Anxiety." *Medical Problems of Performing Artists* 18, no. 3 (September 2003): 126–30.

Chaoul, M. Alejandro, and Lorenzo Cohen. "Rethinking Yoga and the Application of Yoga in Modern Medicine." *CrossCurrents* 60, no. 2 (June 2010): 144–67.

Chapman, Gary. *Anger: Taming a Powerful Emotion*. Chicago: Moody, 2015.

Chemaly, Soraya. *Rage Becomes Her: The Power of Women's Anger*. New York: Atria, 2018.

Cina, Jacy A. "Music Performance Anxiety and Cognitive-Behavioral Therapy: Some Pedagogical Insights." *College Music Symposium* 61, no. 2 (Fall 2021): 53–67.

Clance, P. R., and S. A. Imes. "The Imposter Phenomenon in High Achieving Women: Dynamics and Therapeutic Intervention." *Psychotherapy: Theory, Research, and Practice* 15, no. 3 (1987): 241–7.

Clark, Duncan B., and W. Stewart Agras. "The Assessment and Treatment of Performance Anxiety in Musicians." *The American Journal of Psychiatry* 148, no. 5 (May 1991): 598–605.

Cleveland Clinic. "Acceptance and Commitment Therapy." September 30, 2024. https://my.clevelandclinic.org/health/treatments/acceptance-and-commitment-therapy-act-therapy (accessed March 19, 2025).

Cleveland Clinic. "Amygdala." April 11, 2023. https://my.clevelandclinic.org/health/body/24894-amygdala (accessed March 15, 2025).

Cleveland Clinic. "Autonomic Nervous System." June 15, 2022. https://my.clevelandclinic.org/health/body/23273-autonomic-nervous-system (accessed March 16, 2025).

Cleveland Clinic. "Frontal Lobe." December 5, 2022. https://my.clevelandclinic.org/health/body/24501-frontal-lobe (accessed March 15, 2025).

Cleveland Clinic. "Hippocampus." May 14, 2024. https://my.clevelandclinic.org/health/body/hippocampus (accessed March 15, 2025).

Cleveland Clinic. "Norepinephrine (Noradrenaline)." March 27, 2022. https://my.clevelandclinic.org/health/articles/22610-norepinephrine-noradrenaline (accessed March 19, 2025).

Cleveland Clinic. "What is the Flight, Fight, Freeze, or Fawn Response?" July 22, 2024. https://health.clevelandclinic.org/what-happens-to-your-body-during-the-fight-or-flight-response (accessed March 20, 2025).

Cosgrove, Mark. *Counseling For Anger*. Dallas: Word Publishing, 1988.

Cron, Ian Morgan, and Suzanne Stabile. *The Road Back to You: An Enneagram Journey to Self-Discovery*. Downers Grove: InterVarsity Press, 2016.

Dobson, Debora, and Keith S. Dobson. *Evidence-Based Practice of Cognitive-Behavioral Therapy*. New York: Guilford Press, 2009.

Dovey, Ceridwen. "Can Reading Make You Happier?" *New Yorker*, June 9, 2015. https://www.newyorker.com/culture/cultural-comment/can-reading-make-you-happier (accessed February 12, 2024).

Doyle, Glennon, host. "Enneagram: Why You Are the Way You Are with Suzanne Stabile." *We Can Do Hard Things*, episode 226a, July 10, 2023, Audacy. https://momastery.com/blog/we-can-do-hard-things-ep-226/ (accessed February 20, 2024).

Doyle, Glennon, host. "Fix Your Most Important Relationships with the Enneagram: Suzanne Stabile." *We Can Do Hard Things*, episode 226b, July 11, 2023, Audacy. https://momastery.com/blog/we-can-do-hard-things-ep-bonus-2/ (accessed February 20, 2024).

Duckworth, Angela. *Grit: The Power of Passion and Perseverance*. New York: Scribner, 2016.

Duffy, Thomas. *A+: A Precise Prelude and an Excellent March*. https://www.duffymusic.com/a-a-precise-prelude-and-an-excellent-march.html (accessed March 5, 2024).

Eid, Dody. "Divisions of the Brain: Forebrain, Midbrain, Hindbrain." *Simply Psychology*. https://www.simplypsychology.org/forebrain-midbrain-hindbrain.html (accessed March 15, 2025).

Enneagram Institute, The. https://www.enneagraminstitute.com/the-traditional-enneagram/ (accessed March 16, 2025).

Fishbein, Martin, Susan E. Middlestadt, Victor Otttati, Susan Straus, and Alan Ellis. "Medical Problems Among ICSOM Musicians: Overview of a National Survey." *Medical Problems of Performing Artists* 3, no. 1 (March 1988): 1–8.

Fridman, Lex, host. "Andrew Huberman: Relationships, Drama, Betrayal, Sex, and Love." *Lex Fridman Podcast,* episode 393, August 17, 2023. https://lexfridman.com/andrew-huberman-4/ (accessed March 14, 2024).

Funkenstein, Daniel H. "The Physiology of Fear and Anger." *Scientific American* 192, no. 5 (May 1955): 74–81.

Gaylin, Willard. *The Rage Within: Anger in Modern Life.* New York: Simon and Schuster, 1984.

Gillen-O'Neel, Cari, Virginia W. Huyna, and Andrew J. Fuligni. "To Study or Sleep? The Academic Cost of Extra Studying at the Expense of Sleep." *Child Development* 84, no. 1 (January–February 2013): 133–42.

Gómez-López, Belén, and Roberto Sánchez-Cabrero. "Current Trends in Music Performance Anxiety Intervention." *Behavioral Science* 13 (2023): 720.

Green, Barry, and W. Timothy Gallwey. *The Inner Game of Music.* New York: Doubleday, 1986.

Greene, Don. *Fight Your Fear and Win.* New York: Broadway Books, 2001.

Guy-Evans, Olivia. "Motor Cortex: Function and Location." *Simply Psychology.* https://www.simplypsychology.org/motor-cortex.html (accessed March 15, 2025).

Hibberd, Jessamy. *The Imposter Cure: How to Stop Feeling Like a Fraud and Escape the Mind-Trap of Imposter Syndrome.* London: Aster, 2019.

Hoffman, Brian B. *Adrenaline.* Cambridge, MA: Harvard University Press, 2013.

Huberman, Andrew, host. "Dr. Mark D'Esposito: How to Optimize Cognitive Function & Brain Health." *Huberman Lab,* episode 164, February 19, 2024, Scicomm Media. https://www.hubermanlab.com/episode/dr-mark-desposito-how-to-optimize-cognitive-function-brain-health (accessed February 26, 2024).

Huberman, Andrew, host. "Erasing Fears and Traumas Based on the Modern Neuroscience of Fear." *Huberman Lab*, episode 49, December 6, 2021, Scicomm Media. https://www.hubermanlab.com/episode/erasing-fears-and-traumas-based-on-the-modern-neuroscience-of-fear (accessed March 3, 2024).

Huberman, Andrew, host. "Tools for Managing Stress and Anxiety." *Huberman Lab,* episode 10, March 8, 2021, Scicomm Media. https://www.hubermanlab.com/episode/tools-for-managing-stress-and-anxiety (accessed February 27, 2024).

Hunnes, Dana Ellis. "What Are Adaptogens and the Possible Benefits of Taking Them?" *UCLA Fielding School of Public Health*, February 16, 2022. https://www.uclahealth.org/news/what-are-adaptogens-and-should-you-be-taking-them (accessed February 24, 2024).

IFS Institute. "What is Internal Family Systems?" https://ifs-institute.com (accessed March 15, 2025).

Johnson, Gertrude Parker, and Brenda Crispell Johanson. "ß Blockers." *The American Journal of Nursing* 83, no. 7 (July 1983): 1034–43.

Kenny, Dianna T. "Negative Emotions in Music Making: Performance Anxiety." In *Handbook of Music and Emotion: Theory, Research, Applications*, edited by P. Juslin and J. Sloboda, 425–51. Oxford: Oxford University Press, 2010.

Kenny, Dianna T. *The Psychology of Music Performance Anxiety*. Oxford: Oxford University Press, 2011.

Kulkarni, Jayashri. "Perimenopausal Depression–An Under-Recognised Entity." *Australian Prescriber* 41, no. 6 (December 2018): 183–5.

LeBlanc, Albert. "A Theory of Music Performance Anxiety." *The Quarterly* 5, no. 4 (Winter 1994): 60–8.

LeBlanc, Albert, Young Chang Jin, Mary Obert, and Carolyn Siivola. "Effect of Audience on Music Performance Anxiety." *Journal of Research in Music Education* 45, no. 3 (Autumn 1997): 480–96.

Lewin, Naomi, host. "Musicians Use Beta Blockers as Performance-Enabling Drugs." *Conducting Business*, August 16, 2013, WQXR. https://www.wqxr.org/story/312920-musicians-use-beta-blockers-relieve-stage-fright/# (accessed March 1, 2024).

Lonsdale, C., and J. T. Tam. "On the Temporal and Behavioural Consistency of Pre-Performance Routines: An Intra-Individual Analysis of Elite Basketball Players' Free Throw Shooting Accuracy." *Journal of Sports Sciences* 26, no. 3 (2008): 259–66.

McKowen, Laura. *We Are the Luckiest: The Surprising Magic of a Sober Life*. Novato: New World Library, 2020.

Palmer, Parker J. *The Courage to Teach: Exploring the Inner Landscape of a Teacher's Life*. 10th ed. San Francisco: Wiley, 2007.

Riso, Don Richard, and Russ Hudson. *Discovering Your Personality Type: The Essential Introduction to the Enneagram*. Boston: Houghton Mifflin, 2003.

Riso, Don Richard, and Russ Hudson. *Understanding the Enneagram: The Practical Guide to Personality Types*. New York: Houghton Mifflin, 2000.

Ristad, Eloise. *A Soprano on Her Head*. Moad: Real People Press, 1982.

Sachs, Nicole. *The Cure for Chronic Pain.* https://www.thecureforchronicpain.com/anxietycourseintro (accessed March 13, 2024).

Sarno, John E. *The Mindbody Prescription: Healing the Body, Healing the Pain.* New York: Grand Central Life & Style, 1998.

Schouwenburg, H. C. "Academic Procrastination: Theoretical Notions, Measurements, and Research." In *Procrastination and Task Avoidance: Theory, Research, and Treatment* edited by J. R. Ferrari, J. L. Johnson, and W. G. McCown, 71–96. New York: Plenum, 1995.

Schwartz, Richard. *Introduction to Internal Family Systems.* 2nd ed. Boulder: Sounds True, 2023.

Senyshyn, Yaroslav. "Perspectives on Performance and Anxiety and Their Implications for Creative Teaching." *Canadian Journal of Education* 24, no. 1 (1999): 30–41.

Skidmore, Jon, Rob Shallenberger, and Steven Shallenberger. *Conquer Anxiety.* 2020.

Stabile, Suzanne. *The Journey Toward Wholeness: Enneagram Wisdom for Stress, Balance, and Transformation.* Westmont: InterVarsity Press, 2021.

Stabile, Suzanne. *The Path Between Us: An Enneagram Journey to Healthy Relationships.* Downers Grove: InterVarsity Press, 2018.

Stohrer, Sharon L. *The Empowered Performer.* Sharon L. Stohrer, 2022.

Tracy, Brian. *Eat that Frog!: 21 Great Ways to Stop Procrastination and Get More Done in Less Time.* Oakland: Berrett-Koehler, 2017.

Trivedi, Gunjan, Kamal Sharma, Banshi Saboo, Soundappan Kathirvel, Ashwati Konat, Vatsal Zapadia, Poonjan J. Prajapati, Urva Benani, Kahan Patel, and Suchi Shah. "Humming (Simple Bhramari Pranayama) as a Stress Buster: A Holter-Based Study to Analyze Heart Rate Variability (HRV) Parameters During Bhramari, Physical Activity, Emotional Stress, and Sleep." *Cureus* 15, no. 4 (2023): e37527. https://doi.org/10.7759/cureus.37527.

U.S. Congress, Substance Abuse and Mental Health Services Administration. *Cannabidiol (CBD) – Potential Harms, Side Effects and Unknowns.* February 2023, PEP22-06-04-003, Rockville.

Williams, Simon. "Counting Sleep." *RSA Journal* 159, no. 5555 (2013): 36–9.

# Index

adolescence  1, 5, 35, 128
adrenaline  1, 11–13, 21, 25, 40, 70, 82, 87, 133–4, 139, 146
anger  40, 47, 60, 79–92, 95, 99–100, 105, 110–14, 146–8
  defusing anger  40, 85–90, 142
  and health  83–90
anxiety  41, 52–60, 66–7, 69, 79, 83, 87, 90, 96–108, 110, 116, 118–30, 133, 139–40, 146–8
  fight-flight-freeze response  10–13, 40, 66, 82, 146
  parasympathetic & sympathetic responses  11, 107, 139–41
  symptoms of  2, 21, 40, 109–10, 119
brain  8, 24–6, 32, 66, 105–11, 138, 146
  divisions of  5–11
  limbic system  9–11
depression  2, 26, 34, 73, 83, 87, 126, 128–30
enneagram  39–41, 61–2, 68–9, 77–8, 101–6, 110, 112, 133–4, 142, 146–7
  the Achiever  43, 46–60, 96–7
  the Challenger  45–7, 79–92, 99–100
  the Enthusiast  45–7, 63–7, 70–4, 76, 99
  the Helper  42–3, 46–60, 81, 96
  the Individualist  44, 46–52, 54–60, 97–8
  the Investigator  44, 46–7, 63–7, 70–1, 74–6, 97–8, 134
  the Loyalist  44–7, 63–7, 70–6, 98
  the Peacemaker  45–7, 79–92, 100
  the Reformer  42–3, 47, 79–96
fear  10, 12, 29, 31, 41, 43–7, 54, 63–79, 82–3, 87, 95, 97–100, 110, 113, 146–8
fiction  33–4, 60, 137
gender  54, 84, 127–9
hierarchical relationships  123–6
hormones  11–12, 66, 87, 129
  menopause  127–9
Imposter syndrome  40, 47, 54, 56, 60, 96
interrupters  140–1. *See also* physiological sigh
journaling  53, 58–60, 68–71, 74, 76–7, 90, 96, 99, 147
logging  70, 135–7
  courage  69–74, 77
  fear  69–72, 74, 77, 147
  mistakes/errors  135–7
medication  3, 17–25, 29, 35–6, 60, 96, 141–2, 148
  beta-blockers  18–25, 28–9, 35
mind-body connection  141–2, 147. *See also* psychogenic/psychosomatic pain
motivation  42, 46, 58–9, 89, 96–8, 101–6, 141, 145, 147
pandemic/COVID  26–7, 126
perfectionism  43, 46, 54, 56, 96, 113, 120–2, 124, 130
physical exercise  59, 76, 91, 99, 133–4, 137, 142
physiological sigh  91, 138–42, 146

practice  8, 10, 17, 72–4, 96, 99, 102, 107, 115, 122, 127, 133–9, 141–3, 146–9. *See also* logging; journaling
mental practice  76, 114–15, 137–8, 146–7
practice mapping  72–4
procrastination  72–4, 77, 142
psychogenic/psychosomatic pain  84, 108–11, 147
rage  40, 80, 83–9, 111–13, 116–17, 147. *See also* anger
reframing  31, 72, 76, 98, 116–17, 147. *See also* visualization
shame  20, 40, 47, 49–60, 79–80, 90, 95–7, 105, 110, 113, 116, 146–8
sleep  34–5, 100, 107–8, 116, 138–9

social connection  105–6
spiritual practices  140–6
  meditation  17, 32–5, 60, 75, 96, 100, 114, 141–2
  prayer beads  33, 40, 104, 142
  yoga  18, 23, 32, 35, 60, 75–6, 91, 134
therapy  1, 17–8, 26–31, 35, 55, 60, 68–9, 76, 92, 96, 107, 109, 114, 138, 147–8
  Cognitive-Behavioral Therapy  1, 27–31
trauma  27–30, 35, 67–76, 97, 105, 112–13, 117, 147
visualization  3, 17, 31, 34, 76, 98, 114–17, 137–8, 147